Beliefs and Expectancies in Legal Decision Making

Beliefs and expectancies influence our everyday thoughts, feelings, and actions. These attributes make a closer examination of beliefs and expectancies worthwhile in any context, but particularly so within the high-stakes arena of the legal system. Whether the decision maker is a police officer assessing the truthfulness of an alibi, a juror evaluating the accuracy of an eyewitness identification, an attorney arguing a case involving a juvenile offender, or a judge deciding whether to terminate parental rights – these decisions matter and without doubt are influenced by beliefs and expectancies. This volume is comprised of research on beliefs and expectancies regarding alibis, children's behaviour while testifying, eyewitness testimony, confessions, sexual assault victims, judges' decisions in child protection cases, and attorneys' beliefs about jurors' perceptions of juvenile offender culpability. Areas for future research are identified, and readers are encouraged to discover new ways that beliefs and expectancies operate in the legal system.

This book was originally published as a special issue of *Psychology, Crime & Law*.

Bradley D. McAuliff, JD, PhD, is Professor of Psychology at California State University, Northridge, USA. He is Associate Editor of the journal *Law & Human Behavior.*

Brian H. Bornstein, PhD, is Professor of Psychology and Courtesy Professor of Law at the University of Nebraska–Lincoln, USA. He is co-Editor of the journal *Psychology, Crime & Law.*

Beliefs and Expectancies in Legal Decision Making

Edited by
Bradley D. McAuliff and
Brian H. Bornstein

Routledge
Taylor & Francis Group

LONDON AND NEW YORK

First published 2015 by Routledge

2 Park Square, Milton Park, Abingdon, Oxon, OX14 4RN
605 Third Avenue, New York, NY 10017

Routledge is an imprint of the Taylor & Francis Group, an informa business

First issued in paperback 2020

British Library Cataloguing in Publication Data
A catalogue record for this book is available from the British Library

ISBN 13: 978-1-138-80959-8 (hbk)
ISBN 13: 978-0-367-73990-4 (pbk)

Typeset in Times New Roman
by RefineCatch Limited, Bungay, Suffolk

Publisher's Note
The publisher accepts responsibility for any inconsistencies that may have
arisen during the conversion of this book from journal articles to book chapters,
namely the possible inclusion of journal terminology.

Disclaimer
Every effort has been made to contact copyright holders for their permission to
reprint material in this book. The publishers would be grateful to hear from any
copyright holder who is not here acknowledged and will undertake to rectify
any errors or omissions in future editions of this book.

Contents

Contents

Citation Information

The chapters in this book were originally published in *Psychology, Crime & Law*, volume 18, numbers 1–2 (January–February 2012). When citing this material, please use the original page numbering for each article, as follows:

Chapter 7
Terminating parental rights: the relation of judicial experience and expectancy-related factors to risk perceptions in child protection cases
Alicia Summers, Sophia Gatowski and Shirley Dobbin
Psychology, Crime & Law, volume 18, numbers 1–2 (January–February 2012) pp. 95–112

Chapter 8
Attorney and lay beliefs about factors affecting jurors' perceptions of juvenile offender culpability
Catherine R. Camilletti and Matthew H. Scullin
Psychology, Crime & Law, volume 18, numbers 1–2 (January–February 2012) pp. 113–128

Please direct any queries you may have about the citations to
clsuk.permissions@cengage.com

Notes on Contributors

Bradley D. McAuliff, Department of Psychology, California State University, Northridge, USA

Brian H. Bornstein, Department of Psychology, University of Nebraska–Lincoln, USA

Catherine R. Camilletti, Department of Psychology, University of Texas at El Paso, El Paso, USA

Ashley Christiansen, Department of Psychology, University of Nebraska–Lincoln, Lincoln, Nebraska, USA

Shirley Dobbin, Systems Change Solutions, Inc., White Rock, B.C., Canada

Jennifer E. Dysart, Department of Psychology, John Jay College of Criminal Justice, New York, USA

Jacqueline R. Evans, Department of Psychology, University of Texas at El Paso, El Paso, Texas, USA

Sophia Gatowski, Systems Change Solutions, Inc., White Rock, B.C., Canada

Allyson J. Horgan, Department of Psychology, University of Texas at El Paso, El Paso, Texas, USA

Marc A. Klippenstine, East Central University, Ada, Oklahoma, USA

Margaret Bull Kovera, John Jay College of Criminal Justice, New York, USA

Christian A. Meissner, Department of Psychology, University of Texas at El Paso, El Paso, Texas, USA

Tess M.S. Neal, Department of Psychology, The University of Alabama, Tuscaloosa, AL, USA

Timothy R. Robicheaux, Department of Psychology, The Pennsylvania State University, University Park, Pennsylvania, USA

Melissa B. Russano, Roger Williams University, Bristol, Rhode Island, USA

Regina Schuller, York University, Toronto, Ontario, Canada

Matthew H. Scullin, Department of Psychology, University of Texas at El Paso, El Paso, USA

NOTES ON CONTRIBUTORS

Alicia Summers, National Council of Juvenile and Family Court Judges, Reno, Nevada, USA

Deryn Strange, Department of Psychology, John Jay College of Criminal Justice, New York, USA

Beliefs and expectancies in legal decision making: an introduction

Bradley D. McAuliff[a] and Brian H. Bornstein[b]

[a]*Department of Psychology, California State University, Northridge;* [b]*Department of Psychology, University of Nebraska-Lincoln*

This introduction describes what the co-editors believe readers can expect in this Special Issue. After beliefs and expectancies are defined, examples of how these constructs influence human thought, feeling, and behavior in legal settings are considered. Brief synopses are provided for the Special Issue papers on beliefs and expectancies regarding alibis, children's testimony behavior, eyewitness testimony, confessions, sexual assault victims, judges' decisions in child protection cases, and attorneys' beliefs about jurors' perceptions of juvenile offender culpability. Areas for future research are identified, and readers are encouraged to discover new ways that beliefs and expectancies operate in the legal system.

We are pleased to introduce this Special Issue of *Psychology, Crime, & Law* on beliefs and expectancies in legal decision making. The catalyst for this collaboration was a series of conference-situated musings between a social psychologist and cognitive psychologist about two pillars of human behavior: beliefs and expectancies. Beliefs and expectancies are at once both mundane and extraordinary. Mundane in the sense that they undergird all human behavior; something each and every one of us experiences each and every day. Yet they are equally, if not even more, extraordinary when we consider the far-reaching implications of how they directly link to our thoughts, feelings, and actions. These attributes make a closer examination of beliefs and expectancies worthwhile in any context, but particularly so within the high-stakes arena of the legal system. Whether the decision maker is a police officer assessing the truthfulness of an alibi, a juror evaluating the accuracy of an eyewitness identification, an attorney arguing a case involving a juvenile offender, or a judge deciding whether to terminate parental rights—these decisions matter and without doubt are influenced by beliefs and expectancies.

The purpose of this Introduction is to inform readers what we believe they should expect in the Special Issue. We begin by defining what we mean by beliefs and expectancies and then consider some of the ways these constructs influence our thoughts, feelings, and behavior in legal settings. Next, we provide brief synopses of the articles contained herein and conclude by encouraging readers to investigate exciting new ways that beliefs and expectancies shape legal decision making.

Beliefs and expectancies defined

It is only fitting that we begin by defining what we mean by beliefs and expectancies. Beliefs are bits of information or knowledge that are subjectively accepted as true and often involve links between an object/target and an attribute (Fishbein & Ajzen, 1975). We form beliefs primarily based on personal experience and communication with other people. One might believe, for example, that this year's Nebraska Cornhuskers are the greatest college football team ever or that the goldenrod is the prettiest flower on earth. Here we see particular objects (a football team and a flower) linked to specific attributes (athletic prowess and beauty). Note that although the attributes listed here are positive, they need not necessarily be (football teams can be bad and flowers can be ugly). Valence aside, the key for a belief is that the information or link is thought to be true—whether or not it factually *is* true—and, as such, serves as a springboard for expectancies.

Expectancies are beliefs about a future state of affairs (Olson, Roese, & Zanna, 1996). They entail subjective estimates of likelihood, ranging from a mere possibility to a virtual certainty (Roese & Sherman, 2007). The relative certainty and valence of expectancies can vary based on individual and situational factors. Returning to our previous example, one's belief about the athletic prowess of the Cornhuskers may lead a person to expect the team will likely win its football game this weekend, just as one's belief about the beauty of goldenrods may lead a person to expect that if he gives a goldenrod bouquet to his sweetheart, she probably will be delighted. Although these examples refer to explicit or conscious expectancies, implicit expectancies operate in our daily lives as well. For instance, I turn the key in my car ignition every day expecting the engine to start without explicitly thinking about this outcome. As simple as these examples might appear, we hope they make the following points clear: (1) not all beliefs are expectancies; (2) expectancies are predicated on beliefs ('My belief about X leads me to expect Y'); (3) expectancies are future-oriented; and (4) some expectancies are more factually accurate than others.

Beliefs and expectancies in legal decision making

Much can and has been said about how beliefs and expectancies influence our everyday thoughts, feelings, and actions (see Miller & Turnbull, 1986, for a review). We have chosen to narrow the focus for the Special Issue by examining how these constructs operate within the legal system. Beliefs and expectancies affect how we think by guiding what we attend to, encode, and remember in the world around us (Roese & Sherman, 2007). We actively tend to seek out information that confirms (rather than disconfirms) our pre-existing beliefs and expectancies (Lord, Ross, & Lepper, 1979). Social and cognitive psychologists refer to this tendency as a 'confirmation bias', and applied psychologists have repackaged it as 'experimenter bias', 'investigator bias', and 'interviewer bias'. The gist of this concept is captured by the colloquialisms 'Seek and ye shall find' and 'What we see is what we expect'. Whether actors are fans from rival athletic teams (Hastorf & Cantril, 1954), students evaluating a professor (Kelley, 1950), bystanders witnessing an ambiguous shove (Duncan, 1976), or an experimenter testing a hypothesis (Rosenthal, 1976), people tend to interpret information in line with their previously held beliefs and expectancies. This tendency has direct implications for anyone involved in the legal system. A police officer's determination of a suspect's truthfulness, a forensic examiner's evaluation of a defendant's competency, or a juror's assessment of a witness's credibility, are but a few examples of how beliefs and expectancies impact legal outcomes. Suspects may be released or detained, defendants may be tried or committed, and witnesses may be believed or discarded in a biased fashion. According to this perspective, knowing a person's beliefs or expectancies should provide valuable information when attempting to predict or understand legal decision making.

Beliefs and expectancies guide our behavior in addition to influencing how we think. Of particular concern is that we tend to behave in ways that elicit the outcomes we expect. Psychologists have used various labels to describe this phenomenon, such as 'expectancy effects', 'self-fulfilling prophecy', and 'behavioral confirmation'. The behaviors involved can vary along several dimensions. They may be verbal or nonverbal, deliberate or unintentional, and positive or negative. They may exert influence alone or in concert with one another. Early research by Rosenthal and his colleagues documented expectancy effects in classroom and laboratory settings. Elementary students randomly labeled as 'bloomers' and rats randomly labeled as 'maze smart' outperformed their counterparts when teachers and experimenters were told these labels in advance (Rosenthal, 1976; Rosenthal & Jacobson, 1968). In essence, the labels caused teachers/experimenters to behave in ways that facilitated outcomes consistent with their beliefs and expectancies (i.e., better grades and faster maze times).

Similar findings have emerged on tasks more directly related to the legal system such as eyewitness lineup identifications and suspect interrogations. In fact, one could argue that expectancy effects are even more likely to occur in this setting, given the significance of the decisions being made (crime investigation, determination of guilt/innocence, terminating parental rights, sentencing) and the firmly-held convictions of the parties involved (police officers, corrections officers, forensic interviewers, experts, judges, and attorneys). Investigator bias can arise in eyewitness identification lineups when the lineup administrator knows the identity of the suspect (who may or may not be the actual perpetrator). Compared to double-blind lineups in which neither the administrator nor the eyewitness knows the suspect's identity, single-blind lineups in which the administrator knows the suspect's identity result in higher identification rates of the suspect (Greathouse & Kovera, 2009; Haw & Fisher, 2004; Phillips, McAuliff, Kovera, & Cutler, 1999), higher levels of eyewitness confidence in the identification decision (Garrioch & Brimacombe, 2001), and differences in the verbal and nonverbal behavior of the lineup administrator (Greathouse & Kovera, 2009). Even more troubling, eyewitnesses and lineup administrators report few if any differences in administrator influence as a function of the single- versus double-blind procedure (Greathouse & Kovera, 2009; Phillips et al., 1999). Either they are unaware of the bias or simply refuse to report it.

Researchers studying interrogations and confessions have found that interrogators who are led to believe the suspect is guilty tend to ask more guilt-presumptive questions, use tougher interrogation tactics, and exert more pressure on suspects to get a confession than those who are led to believe the suspect is innocent (Kassin, Goldstein, & Savitsky, 2003). Interestingly, the effect of this interrogator bias is not the same for suspects who are truly guilty versus truly innocent; the bias increases the likelihood of confessions by innocent suspects, but has no effect on the likelihood of confessions from guilty suspects (Narchet, Meissner, & Russano, 2011). Breaking this process down, we can see that an innocent suspect is more likely to confess when the interrogator believes the suspect is guilty because this belief leads the interrogator to behave differently during the interrogation, which in turn elicits behavior from the suspect (a confession) that confirms the interrogator's initial (and in this case, incorrect) belief.

Why do beliefs and expectancies exert such a strong influence on the behavior of others? One potential mechanism is demand characteristics, which refer to the totality of cues present in a situation that convey the expected or desired outcome to an individual (Orne, 1962). Whereas expectancy effects are rooted in the motives of the actor, demand characteristics depend on the perceptions of the individual in the situation with the actor. Wells and Luus (1990) extended Orne's original work on demand characteristics in psychological experiments to eyewitness identification lineups by likening an investigator to an experimenter and an eyewitness to a participant. Much like participants in experiments want to provide the experimenter 'good data', witnesses are motivated to do the same for investigators for several reasons.

One reason is altruism, which motivates people to do what they believe is good or right in a given situation. Just as a participant wants to contribute to a successful experiment by confirming the experimenter's hypothesis, so too does a victim or witness during a lineup/interview want to help by providing whatever information is expected by the investigator. This information may consist of details about an alleged crime or the identification of a suspect from a photo lineup. Child witnesses are particularly susceptible to subtle (and sometimes not-so-subtle) expectancies conveyed by the interviewer as to what the 'right' answer is, leading them, for example, to be more likely to change their answer when asked the same question multiple times (e.g., Ceci & Friedman, 2000).

Evaluation apprehension is a second reason why participants are sensitive to demand characteristics in experiments and other situations (Orne, 1962). We seek to generate favorable impressions of ourselves in others, and one way to do so is to comply with the perceived goals or expectancies of others in a situation. In experiments, participants desire to win the approval of the experimenter and attempt to maximize the positive aspects of their evaluation while minimizing any negative aspects (Rosenthal & Rosnow, 1991). Victims and witnesses may behave similarly in legal contexts. Evaluation apprehension may be reflected in the tendency of inaccurate eyewitnesses to provide more detailed explanations of their identification process ('I compared the photos to each other to narrow the choices') than accurate eyewitnesses (Dunning & Stern, 1994). Essentially, they want to appear like a 'good eyewitness' to gain the approval of the investigator. The need for positive evaluation also might help explain why affirming post-identification feedback from an investigator (e.g., 'Good, you identified the suspect') causes eyewitnesses to overestimate the positive aspects of the witnessing experience, including their certainty, quality of view, clarity of memory, and attention during the event (Wells & Bradfield, 1998).

Obedience to authority is a third reason why people are motivated to comply with demand characteristics. In a psychological experiment, this refers to participants' desire to do what is asked of them because they see the experimenter as an authority figure who should be obeyed (Rosenthal & Rosnow, 1991). A classic example of this phenomenon is Milgram's (1963) study of obedience to authority in which participants were willing to administer dangerously high levels of an electrical shock to another person simply because the experimenter encouraged them to do so. High stress and situation unfamiliarity may exacerbate deference to authority figures as well—attributes that some would argue characterize any interaction with law enforcement or other members of the legal system. Like experimenters, legal professionals must be cognizant of and vigilant against the influence of demand characteristics arising from altruism, evaluation apprehension, and obedience to authority.

Finally, much like beliefs and expectancies influence our thoughts and behavior, they affect our feelings as well. We react negatively to information that disconfirms our pre-existing beliefs and expectancies (Olson et al., 1996). Some researchers have argued that this negative affective state is caused by the disruption of processing fluency (Winkielman & Cacioppo, 2001). In other words, we do not like having to expend the additional cognitive resources required to reconcile disconfirming information or experiences. Another possible explanation involves the false consensus effect, which states that we tend to overestimate the degree to which others agree with us (Marks & Miller, 1987). If false consensus is psychologically comforting and self-validating, then the exact opposite may be true when we realize that others do not share our beliefs or expectancies. Simply put, disconfirming evidence yields an unpleasant, negative affective state that we seek to reduce, eliminate, or avoid altogether. The emotional effects of expectancy confirmation or disconfirmation are especially relevant for jurors evaluating witness behavior in court (Bornstein & Greene, 2011), but we can see how they might affect other actors in the legal system too. For example, imagine a forensic interviewer who believes a child was sexually abused based on information provided by a school counselor. She might experience frustration or other negative emotions if the child provides information that is inconsistent with what she believes happened. This negative emotional reaction could bleed into her verbal and nonverbal behavior (how she asks questions/responds to answers), which in turn could influence the child's responses as a function of demand characteristics. The end result could be a child alleging abuse that did not occur.

To summarize, beliefs and expectancies influence how we think, feel, and behave in essentially all situations, not excepting those presumed to be purely objective and dispassionate, such as legal contexts (Bornstein & Wiener, 2010). In the next section, we provide brief synopses of the papers selected for this Special Issue. Our goals in putting together the Special Issue were twofold: to include research that was novel both in content and approach, and to advance our understanding of beliefs and expectancies in legal decision making.

The Special Issue: a sneak peek

We open with a paper on alibis by Jennifer Dysart and Deryn Strange. Alibi evidence has received increased attention from legal scholars and social scientists in the wake of recent Innocence Project DNA exonerations—some of which involved shaky or nonexistent alibis—and the publication of an alibi typology by Olsen and Wells (2004). Most research to date has focused on jurors' perceptions of alibi believability, yet law enforcement officers and prosecutors must make critical decisions about alibi believability before charging an individual with a crime and proceeding to trial.

In their paper for this Special Issue, Dysart and Strange sought to fill this void in the literature by surveying US and Canadian senior law enforcement personnel about their beliefs and experiences involving alibi evidence. Overall, respondents were quite skeptical of alibis, but they believed that investigating alibis sooner rather than later increases their utility in determining a suspect's potential criminal involvement. The most believable alibi stories include physical evidence or a statement from an unmotivated other, but those occur only in a minority of cases. These survey findings shed light on an important, but heretofore overlooked, population with respect to alibi evidence. Whether prosecutors and, ultimately, jurors share similar beliefs and concerns about alibis remains an unanswered research question ripe for investigation.

Many states have introduced evidentiary and procedural innovations to help facilitate children's testimony in abuse cases. Certain innovations, such as closed-circuit television (CCTV) testimony, reduce children's stress and increase their accuracy; however, jurors tend to evaluate children who use CCTV more negatively on a variety of credibility-related dimensions (Goodman, Tobey, Batterman-Faunce, Orcutt, Thomas, Shapiro, et al., 1998). To better understand this vexing issue, McAuliff and Kovera's paper describes results from a survey in which prospective jurors listed their expectancies for a child's verbal and nonverbal behavior across five different testimony conditions (traditional versus several alternative forms of testimony), as well as their beliefs about discerning children's truthfulness, testimony stress, and fairness to trial parties. Prospective jurors expected a child providing traditional testimony to be more nervous, tearful, and fidgety; less confident, cooperative, and fluent; and to maintain less eye contact and provide shorter responses than when the child provided alternative forms of testimony. They also believed it was easiest to determine a child's truthfulness and fairest to the defendant when the child testified live in court, but that this form of testimony was the most stressful and unfair to the child. If accommodated children remain nervous (and data from actual trials suggest this is so), they may fail to meet jurors' expectancies and be viewed more negatively as a result. Future research that systematically varies the presence or absence of children's expected behaviors is needed to determine how jurors react to expectancy violation, as well as the potential role of legal safeguards in reducing any unintended negative effects.

Eyewitness testimony can be extremely compelling yet imperfect trial evidence. Effectively evaluating such testimony requires that jurors know what factors influence eyewitness accuracy, identify those factors (when present) in a case, and weigh their potential impact on the eyewitness's memory accordingly. This is no small feat, and previous research has shown that laypeople's beliefs about factors that influence eyewitness accuracy are often incorrect (e.g., Boyce, Beaudry, & Lindsay, 2007). Neal, Christiansen, Bornstein, and Robicheaux expand this body of research in two studies examining mock jurors' beliefs about the effects of eyewitness age, weapon presence, and identification decision time on eyewitness accuracy and whether those beliefs predict trial-related decisions. Neal and her colleagues systemically manipulated eyewitness age, weapon presence, and identification decision time in different versions of a robbery-murder case and observed that, to some extent, participants' beliefs about these factors interacted with the manipulations to affect mock jurors' judgments. These findings highlight the continued need for expert testimony on factors that influence eyewitness accuracy. Voir dire surveys that target beliefs about specific factors such as eyewitness age and weapon presence, instead of more general beliefs about eyewitness accuracy, might also be useful to attorneys when selecting a jury in cases involving eyewitness evidence.

Much like alibi and eyewitness evidence, research on confessions has gained considerable momentum in the wake of recent DNA exonerations (for a review, see Kassin, Drizin, Grisso, Gudjonsson, Leo, & Redlich, 2010). Horgan, Russano, Meissner, and Evans present research on the diagnostic value of confessions (i.e., the ratio of true to false confessions elicited) obtained using common minimization (i.e., expectation of leniency) and maximization (i.e., threat of harsher punishment) tactics. The authors used pilot data to identify minimization and maximization tactics believed to influence (or not influence) the expected consequences of confessing and then varied these tactics in a written description of the Russano, Meissner, Narchet, and Kassin (2005) paradigm. Participants were sensitive to the use of manipulative techniques in the interrogation descriptions and believed that such techniques could lead other people (but notably, not themselves) to confess falsely. However, when participants actually engaged in the Russano et al. interrogation paradigm in Study 2, they were vulnerable to the manipulation of consequences and were more likely to provide a false confession as a result. Horgan and her colleagues argue that even though the minimization and maximization tactics used in their studies are technically legal, they might undermine the goal of eliciting true confessions and place innocent suspects at greater risk.

Sexual assault cases often lack corroborative evidence, requiring jurors to discern between two dramatically conflicting accounts from the alleged victim and perpetrator. Judgments of credibility are paramount in this process and draw on laypeople's expectancies for how witnesses should behave while testifying. Researchers have studied the type of emotional reactions decision makers expect from victims, but less is known about the expected consistency of those emotional reactions over time. Klippenstine and Schuller address this lingering issue using a written trial simulation in which they orthogonally manipulated a victim's response (tearful/upset versus calm/controlled) both the day following the alleged sexual assault and then again during her trial testimony. Quite interestingly, mock jurors were more supportive of the victim and less supportive of the accused on multiple measures when the victim's response was consistent over time, irrespective of whether that response was tearful/upset or calm/controlled. These findings raise concern for how a victim who improves her ability to cope over time (perhaps through counseling) may be disadvantaged in the eyes of jurors, given their expectancies for emotional consistency over time.

In cases of substantiated abuse or neglect, children often are removed from the home and placed in foster care. Child protection court judges must make crucial decisions involving the permanency plan for each child. A key consideration in this process is the perceived risk of the child's returning home versus remaining in foster care. Little is known regarding how judges actually determine perceived risk and what information factors into their determinations. For their contribution to this Special Issue, Summers, Gatowsky, and Dobbin surveyed child protection court judges to examine the influence of experience, expectancy-related case information, and other individual factors on their risk perceptions in a simulated termination of parental rights case. Three expectancy-related case factors varied across different versions of the case materials: sibling presence, parental involvement in a support group, and statistical information regarding the child's adoptability. Experienced judges' perceptions of risk were predicted by sibling presence and parental support group involvement, whereas less experienced judges' perceptions were predicted by adoptability statistics and individual factors including negative emotion, cognitive style, and age. Summers and her colleagues argue that less experienced judges may not be adequately equipped to recognize factors relevant to risk perceptions and that increased judicial rotations are necessary to improve judges' understanding of child abuse and neglect cases.

In the final article, Camilletti and Scullin present a survey of attorneys and college students on factors believed to influence jurors' perceptions of juvenile offender culpability. The two samples disagreed about the potential influence of certain factors such as abuse history, race/ethnicity, and poor quality of area schools, but agreed that a juvenile offender's youthful appearance would mitigate his perceived culpability and that juvenile crime trend information would have no effect. Contrary to those beliefs, a follow-up simulation study that manipulated both variables revealed that only juvenile crime trend information affected mock jurors' decisions. These data remind us that what attorneys believe are important mitigating factors for their juvenile clients may or may not correspond with jurors' actual beliefs and decisions in juvenile cases. Defense and prosecuting attorneys would benefit by targeting jurors' beliefs about juvenile crime trends during voir dire in cases involving juvenile offenders.

Conclusions

We hope readers will enjoy the Special Issue and close by encouraging them to consider novel applications of beliefs and expectancies to the legal system. Given the ubiquitous nature of these constructs, there is no shortage of research to be done. Some understudied areas that appear particularly well-suited for examination include jury decision making in civil cases (e.g., expectancies about a 'reasonable' damages award), determinations of probation and parole made within the corrections system, the evaluation and interpretation of forensic evidence (e.g., handwriting, fingerprint, accident reconstruction, and tool mark analysis), attorney indoctrination of jurors during voir dire, and the role of unintentional adversarial allegiance in expert testimony, just to name a few. We look forward to revisiting the topic 10 years from now and pointing to all the great research that has been done—you might even say we expect it.

References

Bornstein, B.H., & Greene, E. (2011). Jury decision making: Implications for and from psychology. *Current Directions in Psychological Science, 20*, 63–67. doi:10.1177/ 0963721410397282

Bornstein, B.H., & Wiener, R.L. (2010). *Emotion and the law: Psychological perspectives.* New York, NY: Springer.

Boyce, M., Beaudry, J., & Lindsay, R.C.L. (2007). Belief of eyewitness identification evidence. In R.C.L. Lindsay, D.F. Ross, J.D. Read, & M.P. Toglia (Eds.), *The handbook of eyewitness psychology: Memory for people* (Vol. 2, pp. 501–525). Mahwah, NJ: Erlbaum.

Ceci, S.J., & Friedman, R.D. (2000). The suggestibility of children: Scientific research and legal implications. *Cornell Law Review, 86*, 33–108.

Duncan, S.L. (1976). Differential social perception and attribution of intergroup violence: Testing the lower limits of stereotyping of blacks. *Journal of Personality and Social Psychology, 34, 590–598.* doi:10.1037/0022-3514.34.4.590

Dunning, D., & Stern, L.B. (1994). Distinguishing accurate from inaccurate eyewitness identification via inquiries about decision processes. *Journal of Personality and Social Psychology, 67,* 818–835. doi:10.1037/0022-3514.67.5.818

Fishbein, M., & Ajzen, I. (1975). *Belief, attitude, intention, and behavior: An introduction to theory and research.* Reading, MA: Addison-Wesley.

Garrioch, L., & Brimacombe (nee Luus), C.A.E. (2001). Lineup administrators' expectations: Their impact on eyewitness confidence. *Law and Human Behavior, 25, 299–314.* doi:10.1023/A:1010750028643

Goodman, G.S., Tobey, A.E., Batterman-Faunce, J.M., Orcutt, H., Thomas, S., Shapiro, C., et al. (1998). Face-to-face confrontation: Effects of closed circuit-technology on children's eyewitness testimony and jurors' decisions. *Law and Human Behavior, 22,* 165–203. doi:10.1023/A:1025742119977

Greathouse, S.M., & Kovera, M.B. (2009). Instruction bias and lineup presentation moderate the effects of administrator knowledge on eyewitness identification. *Law and Human Behavior, 33,* 70–82. doi:10.1007/s10979-008-9136-x

Hastorf, A.H., & Cantril, H. (1954). They saw a game: A case study. *Journal of Abnormal and Social Psychology, 49,* 129–134. doi:10.1037/h0057880

Haw, R.M., & Fisher, R.P. (2004). Effects of administrator-witness contact on eyewitness identification accuracy. *Journal of Applied Psychology, 89,* 1106–1112. doi:10.1037/0021-9010.89.6.1106

Kassin, S., Goldstein, C., & Savitsky, K. (2003). Behavioral confirmation in the interrogation room: On the dangers of presuming guilt. *Law and Human Behavior, 27,* 187–203. doi:10.1023/A:1022599230598

Kassin, S.M., Drizin, S.A., Grisso, T., Gudjonsson, G.H., Leo, R.A., & Redlich, A.D. (2010). Police-induced confessions: Risk-factors and recommendations. *Law and Human Behavior, 34,* 3–38. doi:10.1007/s10979-009-9188-6

Kelley, H.H. (1950). The warm-cold variable in first impressions of people. *Journal of Personality, 18,* 431–439. doi:10.1111/j.1467-6494.1950.tb01260.x

Lord, C.G., Ross, L., & Lepper, M.R. (1979). Biased assimilation and attitude polarization: The effects of prior theories on subsequently considered evidence. *Journal of Personality and Social Psychology, 37,* 2098–2109. doi:10.1037/0022-3514.37.11.2098

Marks, G., & Miller, N. (1987). Ten years of research on the false-consensus effect: An empirical and theoretical review. *Psychological Bulletin, 102,* 72–90. doi:10.1037/0033-2909.102.1.72

Milgram, S. (1963). Behavioral study of obedience. *Journal of Abnormal and Social Psychology, 67,* 371–378. doi:10.1037/h0040525

Miller, D.T., & Turnbull, W. (1986). Expectancies and interpersonal processes. *Annual Review of Psychology, 37,* 233–256. doi:10.1146/annurev.ps.37.020186.001313

Narchet, F.M., Meissner, C.A., & Russano, M.B. (2011). Modeling the influence of investigator bias on the elicitation of true and false confessions. *Law and Human Behavior, 35,* 452–465. doi:10.1007/s10979-010-9257-x

Olsen, E., & Wells, G.L. (2004). What makes a good alibi? A proposed taxonomy. *Law and Human Behavior, 28,* 157–176. doi:10.1023/B:LAHU.0000022320.47112.d3

Olson, J.M., Roese, N.J., & Zanna, M.P. (1996). Expectancies. In E.T. Higgins & A.W. Kruglanski (Eds.), *Social psychology: Handbook of basic principles* (pp. 211–238). New York, NY: Guilford Press.

Orne, M.T. (1962). On the social psychology of the psychological experiment: With particular reference to demand characteristics and their implications. *American Psychologist, 17,* 776–783. doi:10.1037/h0043424

Phillips, M.R., McAuliff, B.D., Kovera, M.B., & Cutler, B.L. (1999). Double-blind photoarray administration as a safeguard against investigator bias. *Journal of Applied Psychology, 84,* 940–951. doi:10.1037/0021-9010.84.6.940

Roese, N.J., & Sherman, J.W. (2007). Expectancy. In A.W. Kruglanski & E.T. Higgins (Eds.), *Social psychology: Handbook of basic principles* (2nd ed., pp. 91–115). New York, NY: Guilford Press.

Rosenthal, R. (1976). *Experimenter effects in behavioral research*. New York, NY: Irvington.

Rosenthal, R., & Jacobson, L. (1968). *Pygmalion in the classroom*. New York, NY: Holt, Rinehart & Winston.

Rosenthal, R., & Rosnow, R.L. (1991). *Essentials of behavioral research: Methods and data analysis*. New York, NY: McGraw-Hill.

Russano, M.B., Meissner, C.M., Narchet, F.M., & Kassin, S.M. (2005). Investigating true and false confessions within a novel experimental paradigm. *Psychological Science, 16, 481–486.* doi:10.1111/j.0956-7976.2005.01560.x

Wells, G.L., & Luus, C.A.E. (1990). Police lineups as experiments: Social methodology as a framework for properly conducted lineups. *Personality and Social Psychology Bulletin, 16,* 106–117. doi:10.1177/0146167290161008

Wells, G.L., & Bradfield, A.L. (1998). 'Good, you identified the suspect': Feedback to eyewitnesses distorts their reports of the witnessing experience. *Journal of Applied Psychology, 83,* 360–376. doi:10.1037/0021-9010.83.3.360

Winkielman, P., & Cacioppo, J.T. (2001). Mind at ease puts a smile on the face: Psychophysiological evidence that processing facilitation elicits positive affect. *Journal of Personality and Social Psychology, 81,* 989–1000. doi:10.1037/0022-3514.81.6.989

Beliefs about alibis and alibi investigations: a survey of law enforcement

Jennifer E. Dysart and Deryn Strange

Department of Psychology, John Jay College of Criminal Justice, New York, USA

To date, the majority of published research on alibis has focused on jurors' perceptions of alibi believability. However in criminal cases, it is often law enforcement officers and prosecutors who make decisions about alibi believability that are critical to whether an individual will be charged with a crime. In the current survey, senior law enforcement personnel were questioned about their opinions and experiences regarding alibi investigations and stories. Respondents consistently reported that 'time' is a critical element related to the believability of an alibi story. Specifically, the sooner an alibi story can be investigated, the greater the likelihood that the alibi story will be useful in determining whether the suspect was involved in the crime. In addition, consistent with prior research (Olson & Wells, 2004), participants indicated that the most believable alibi stories are those that include physical evidence or a statement from an unmotivated other. However, respondents reported that suspects provide leads to physical evidence in only 20% of cases, and that unmotivated strangers lie to police in 12% of cases. Overall, the results of the survey show that law enforcement officers are skeptical of alibi statements.

Introduction

When a police officer asks a criminal suspect 'Where were you and what were you doing at Time X?' the answer – whatever it may be – becomes the suspect's alibi story. According to Olson and Wells (2004), an alibi can generally be defined as a 'plea of having been at the time of the commission of an act elsewhere than at the place of commission.' However, an alibi has various connotations associated with it in legal and criminal settings. It can simply be an individual's claim that he/she was elsewhere during the time a crime was committed, a defense strategy that compels the trier of fact to weigh the claim against other evidence, or a term that is reserved for a corroborated claim so that the person is no longer a police suspect (Burke & Turtle, 2003).

Examining the alibi evidence in relation to the 250+ DNA exoneration cases in the United States (Innocence Project, 2010) reveals that many of the exonerees provided some form of alibi evidence in their criminal case. In fact, of the first 157 DNA exoneration cases, more than 25% involved an alibi provided by the defendant that was not believed (Burke, Turtle, & Olson, 2007). In one particularly shocking case, the suspect's alibi story was that he was incarcerated at the time of the crime. However, in what amounts to a clerical error, his photograph was placed in a lineup and an eyewitness subsequently identified him. As a result of the identification, the case progressed through the system, and he was ultimately convicted (Innocence Project, 2010). Indeed, if we take a slightly different approach, since 100% of the DNA exonerees were not guilty of the crime for which they were convicted, it must be true that *all* were somewhere else at the time of the crime. Put another way, they all had some type of alibi story for the time in question. Therefore, the failure of alibi evidence to exculpate innocent suspects could be considered the leading contributing factor to wrongful conviction in the United States. Thus, understanding how law enforcement personnel investigate alibi stories should provide insight into their understanding of the factors that influence those stories. That goal was the focus of our study.

Alibi research

Speaking to the current state of alibi research, Burke et al. (2007) note that, 'the psychology of alibis is as potentially rich, and yet as barren of data, as the eyewitness field was 30 years ago.' Thus, the field is ripe for scientific inquiry. In a particularly important and groundbreaking contribution to the emerging alibi literature, Olson and Wells (2004) proposed a taxonomy of alibis involving two forms of corroborating evidence: *physical evidence* that they classified into three levels (none, easy to fabricate, and difficult to fabricate) and *person evidence* that they classified into four levels (none, motivated familiar other, non-motivated familiar other, and non-motivated stranger). The taxonomy was designed to measure a continuum of believability: Olson and Wells argue that alibis can range from a completely uncorroborated alibi, to an alibi that is supported by a non-motivated but familiar other (i.e. someone who knows the suspect but is not motivated to lie on their behalf) and is accompanied by physical evidence deemed difficult to fabricate. In the present study, to examine whether or not law enforcement officers have a different perspective, we surveyed experienced law enforcement officers about their opinions, beliefs, and experiences regarding alibi believability for various types of alibis (person and physical).

Alibi evaluation and believability

Importantly, the majority of published alibi studies concentrate on what Olson (2002) calls the *evaluation phase* of the alibi, or the point at which the credibility of the alibi story is determined. The majority of research on alibi believability has examined whether or not potential jurors (e.g. Allison & Brimacombe, 2010; Culhane, & Hosch, 2004; McAllister & Bregman, 1989; Sargent & Bradfield, 2004; Sommers & Douglass, 2007) or mock investigators (Dahl, Brimacombe, & Lindsay, 2009; Olson & Wells, 2004; Sommers & Douglass, 2007) find particular alibi stories or alibi witnesses to be more or less credible, but none have asked actual members of law enforcement. For example, Culhane and Hosch (2004) examined the impact of alibis on juror decision-making by manipulating three different factors: the valence of the alibi witnesses' testimony, the relationship of the alibi witness to the defendant, and the confidence of an eyewitness to the crime. Culhane and Hosch found that defendants were more likely to be found guilty when they knew the alibi witness than when they did not. Moreover, participants rated the alibi witness as more important to their decision-making than either the physical evidence or the eyewitness. As a result, Culhane and Hosch concluded that the best kind of alibi witness is a stranger, someone with no prior relationship to the defendant.

Taking a different approach, Sommers and Douglass (2007) investigated the believability of an alibi in relation to the context in which it was evaluated: a police investigation, a criminal trial, or a control condition that mentioned no context. Participants rated the alibi as being stronger and more believable if it was presented in the context of the police investigation. The researchers inferred that potential jurors have an inherent belief that if a case makes it to trial there is a reason why the alibi should not be trusted. Put another way, if the police had believed the defendant's alibi story, it stands to reason that the case would not have progressed to trial. Thus, discovering which types of alibi stories police find credible is an important step in the early stages of this field.

Mistaken alibis

While a suspect's alibi story may simply be found to be true or false, the underlying reasons why suspects provide false alibis may be complex. In some circumstances, suspects may deliberately lie to mislead police or to protect another individual. However, in other cases, a suspect may simply have been *mistaken* about where they were at a particular time in the past. In a recent study conducted by Olson and Charman (in press), participants were asked to truthfully report their whereabouts for four time periods in the past. Forty-eight hours later, participants were asked to return with evidence of their actual whereabouts. The results showed that over one-third (36%) of participants had been mistaken about their activities.

Indeed, we know from the vast literature on autobiographical memory that people's memories are far from perfect. First, for more than a century we have known that the details associated with a particular experience fade with the passage of time (Ebbinghaus, 1885/1913; Wixted, 2004), even for particularly shocking, emotionally laden, and consequential events. Take just one recent example. Within 24 hours of the twin towers falling on September 11, Talarico and Rubin (2003) asked their participants to write a detailed description of where they were and what they were doing when they learned of the event. In addition, they were required to write about a more benign experience they had had recently. Over the course of 224 days, participants showed a roughly parallel rate of forgetting for both kinds of memories. Put another way, even an event that receives a great deal of rehearsal is prone to decay.

Second, and perhaps the most important finding with regard to alibis, is that we are more likely to encode the details of unusual events and subsequently, we are more likely to accurately recall events that were more detailed at encoding (Brewer, 1988; Friedman, 2004; Skowronski, Betz, Thompson, & Shannon, 1991; Thompson, Skowronski, Larsen, & Betz, 1996). The corollary then is that the likelihood of remembering what you were doing during a discrete time period is inevitably linked to whether there was anything significant about that time period. If there was not anything significant about the time period, then it is highly unlikely that people will be able to accurately recall anything about where they were and what they were doing. In the present study, we asked participants to provide examples of why an individual – suspect or witness – might be *mistaken* about where they were at a particular time (10 minutes vs 1 week ago).

Legal issues pertaining to alibis

Although the rules regarding how and when an alibi can or should be used vary greatly across jurisdictions, most jurisdictions within the United States subscribe to a 'prior notice rule.' In other words, if a defendant plans to present an alibi defense, the prosecution must be notified in advance. Indeed, although the courts may consider a late notice, failure to provide any notice can lead to the exclusion of the alibi evidence from trial (e.g. P. v Brown, 2003; Craig, 1996). The generally accepted rationale for the prior notice rule is that, in providing notice ahead of time, defendants will be less likely to manipulate/manufacture their alibi to fit with the facts of the case presented at trial (Epstein, 1964). The underlying assumption is that the details of an alibi story should not change over time, and if they do change, then there was some intention to deceive on the part of the defendant or alibi provider. In the present study, we asked respondents specific questions about how they viewed suspects whose alibi changed over time.

Current study

In the study we report here, we created a survey to administer to law enforcement officers based on the alibi taxonomy (Olson & Wells, 2004) and the existing alibi literature. The topics included: investigation procedures and training, investigation responsibility (law enforcement vs prosecutors vs defense attorneys), and factors related to mistaken alibi statements or stories. We also asked our participants to provide an example of a (believable) alibi story they had heard over the course of their career, and information about the frequency with which suspects provide alibi stories or claims. In particular, we asked about the frequency with which various types of physical alibi evidence are present in criminal investigations and whether law enforcement officers believe this evidence is generally easy or difficult for a suspect to fabricate. In addition, we asked respondents to estimate what percentage of the time individuals from various groups lie to protect a suspect in a criminal investigation so that we could examine officers' expectations of honesty with regards to alibi stories and investigations.

Method

Participants

One hundred and two senior law enforcement personnel were recruited through a study announcement distributed on various police email list-serves. We also informed the respondents that they could forward the survey link to law enforcement colleagues. Of the 102 participants, 39 completed only the demographic questions and did not respond to any survey items. The data we report here, then, come from 63 participants (57 males, six females) who answered at least one survey question in addition to the demographic questions.

On average, respondents (M age $= 44.2$, SD $= 6.3$) had 20.9 (SD $= 7.0$) years of experience in policing. Indeed, the sample included chiefs (7.9%), deputy chiefs (7.9%), captains (11.1%), lieutenants (30.1%), sergeants (17.5%), and detectives, majors, commanders, and those from other ranks (25.5%). On average, they had been in their current rank for 5.1 years (SD $= 3.5$) and had 9.8 years (SD $= 5.7$) of experience as a patrol officer prior to their promotion. The respondents were from 26 different states and two Canadian provinces and the size of their departments' ranged from 10 to 12 000 sworn officers (SD $= 2527.9$) with a median size of 135 officers.

Materials and procedure

We developed a 30-item survey of alibi beliefs. Prior to disseminating the survey, we asked several high-ranking law enforcement officers in the Northeast United States to review the questions to determine whether they reflected terminology that would be understood by the law enforcement community. The officers' suggestions were incorporated into the final instrument (see items in Appendix 1), which was then posted on SurveyMonkey.com, and the survey link was then emailed to several law enforcement list serves in the United States. The survey items included a combination of forced choice, Likert-type questions, and open-ended responses and it took approximately 30 minutes to complete. The categories of alibi topics covered in the survey – and presented below in the results section – were general alibi questions (pertaining to their personal experience with alibi investigations), investigation procedures and responsibility, alibi frequency and lying (for family, friends, etc.), mistaken alibis, physical alibi evidence, and examples of alibi stories. The coding of the open ended-responses was done by both the first author and a research assistant. In instances where the coders disagreed on a category, it was resolved through discussion.

Results

General alibi questions and alibi example

To assess whether our sample had experience with alibis, we asked respondents to estimate how many times a suspect had provided them with an alibi story. Overall, the respondents had a great deal of experience, however, there was an enormous range, from 'dozens' to 'hundreds of times.' Respondents also estimated that suspects give spontaneous alibi statements to police in 62.4% (SD $= 23.1$) of investigations. Despite these responses, only 23% of respondents indicated that they had received specific training on how to interview alibi witnesses.

To examine the respondents' perceptions of alibi believability, we asked them to describe the most believable alibi story a suspect could give. Consistent with the alibi taxonomy, the most common responses were categorized as, physical evidence (e.g. video, work time card, hospital records, jail records; 63.9%), and statements from multiple witnesses (18.0%) or non-motivated others (e.g. co-workers, church members; 11.5%). In addition, some (6.5%) indicated that multiple sources (e.g. receipt and a witness) would be required before they would be inclined to believe an alibi story. Taken together, the responses pertaining to 'what makes a believable alibi' are consistent with previous alibi research using mock jurors and mock investigators (e.g. Olson & Wells, 2004).

In addition, we asked respondents to provide an example of a suspect's alibi story that they had believed to be true, either on the spot without further investigation, or one that was later verified before they accepted the story. Of the examples provided, four people responded that they had never heard a believable alibi story. The remaining 39 examples were classified into groups based on the total amount of evidence that was presented to the officer before accepting the story: physical evidence only (38.5%), no physical or person evidence presented (25.6%), non-motivated witnesses (10.3%), motivated witnesses (10.3%), both physical evidence and a motivated witness (7.7%), both physical evidence and a non-motivated witness (5.1%), and both motivated and non-motivated witnesses (2.6%).

Several of the examples the respondents offered underscore the importance of a thorough alibi investigation, even if the initial story appears weak. For example, one respondent said:

> In one case the victim believed she may have known the identity of a robbery suspect as possibly being someone she had gone to school with years before. In fact, she picked him out of a year book. However, in checking with the employer based in another city, the suspect had claimed to have been at work at the time of the crime, was on the schedule to have worked at that time, and was placed at work by his boss. In this case it seemed coincidental that this suspect would have been a classmate from years before during the initial investigation. There was no reason to later suspect that the alibi witness, the boss, would have lied to protect the suspect, a long-time employee in good standing.

Another example demonstrates the need for a speedy alibi investigation for suspects who are being truthful:

> The suspect of a domestic assault said that he had already left the residence before the time of the alleged crime. He stated that his mother had picked him up, took him to the Dollar General to buy some toothpaste and checked him into a motel. The suspect had a history of domestic violence so he was arrested and I went back to follow up on his alibi. The motel couldn't give a check in time and the mother while supportive of his alibi could not be very specific about times. I returned to the motel room and found the cash register receipt for the toothpaste in the wastebasket. The receipt was date/time stamped [and] did support the alibi. I returned to the witness (friend of victim) and she recanted.

A third example elucidates the importance of a timely investigation to preserve suspect believability:

> I investigated an assault at a bar (fight) in which a witness recognized the suspect who fled the scene. I went to the alleged suspect's residence and interviewed the suspect. He told me he was not at the bar and there was no evidence that the suspect had been drinking alcohol and there was no evidence that he had been in a fight (injuries). I accepted his story and later learned he had a brother who looked very much like him who was in fact the actual suspect.

Investigation procedures

Little is known about which group of law enforcement officers (patrol vs detectives) is most likely to conduct an alibi investigation. Therefore, we asked respondents what percentage of the time they thought members from these two groups follow-up on a suspect's alibi story. Our results showed that detectives were believed to be significantly more likely (78.7%, SD = 20.6) than patrol officers (33.7%, SD = 28.2), $t(62) = 13.9$, $p < 0.01$, $CI_{0.95}$ [38.5, 51.5] to follow-up on an suspect's alibi. If this reflects a true state-of-affairs, then current police practice is likely to enforce some delay between the time a suspect makes an alibi statement and the follow-up interview with potential alibi witnesses, or the search for physical evidence that could support the alibi.

A second survey item regarding the timing of alibi investigations asked how often a suspect's alibi is thoroughly investigated prior to the preparation of a warrant, or before an arrest is made. Interestingly, less than half of our respondents (49.2%) indicated that a thorough investigation is *always* conducted before a warrant or arrest, 38.1% responded that it is *often* investigated, 7.9% said it is *sometimes*, and 4.8% reported that a suspect's alibi story is *rarely* or *never* investigated prior to an arrest or warrant.

A final 'procedure' item in the survey asked respondents to indicate the percentage of time police officers ask a suspect where they were on a specific day and time (e.g. Where were you on Tuesday, April 4th between 2:00 and 2:30 pm?) versus a broader time frame (e.g. Where were you on Tuesday, April 4th?). This question is of particular relevance given the vast literature on autobiographical memories that clearly demonstrates people are not particularly accurate at remembering what they were doing and where they were at a distant time in the past. The results showed that law enforcement officers are significantly more likely to ask about broad (63.1%, SD = 25.6) compared to specific time frames (51.2%, SD = 32.4), $t(62) = 2.4$, $p = 0.02$, $CI_{0.95} = 2.1, 21.7$.

Investigation responsibility

We reported previously that detectives are believed to be the most likely group to follow-up on an alibi story (78.7% of the time). That finding is also consistent with respondents' responses to a follow-up question, where 95.2% indicated that the lead detective, detectives, or police *should be responsible* for following-up on the story. Seven of these respondents (11.9%) also indicated that the law enforcement individual who received the alibi story should be the one to conduct the follow-up, with one person giving a detailed explanation:

> The responsibility is with the person who first receives the information. The dependability and accuracy of most alibi information is time sensitive. The farther from the incident the investigation is conducted, the greater the likelihood that the true facts, or lies, concerning the alibi may be contaminated by contacts and circumstances.

An additional respondent indicated that it is everyone's responsibility, including the prosecution and the defense, and a lone respondent reported that it was the lone responsibility of the defense to conduct an alibi investigation. Further, although 89.3% of respondents believe that it is substandard police practice when police do not investigate an alibi statement, 46.4% said that the failure to investigate an alibi would not be considered police misconduct. Of course, it is important to note that these kinds of responses possibly reflect individual department or jurisdiction practices and may not be consistent across all departments/jurisdictions.

As a follow-up to the responsibility item, we asked respondents to indicate what percentage of the time specific groups (police, prosecutors, public defenders, and private defense attorneys) *actually* investigate alibi stories. Interestingly, although the majority of respondents had earlier reported that they believe police are *responsible* for conducting alibi investigations, the result of this item suggests police do so only 75.8% (SD = 20.5) of the time. When asked how often attorneys investigate alibi statements, private defense attorneys led the group (71.7%, SD = 27.8), followed by public defense attorneys (48.9%, SD = 30.7), and prosecutors (41.5%, SD = 33.9). Finally, although only one respondent indicated that it is the defense's *responsibility* (rather than the police) to investigate a suspect's alibi, 76.8% of respondents believe that when a defense attorney fails to conduct an alibi investigation it constitutes substandard defense lawyering. Prosecutors, on the other hand, who do not investigate a defendant's alibi are judged less harshly; only 46.4% of respondents believe this would constitute prosecutorial misconduct.

Alibi frequency and lying

Given that our respondents reported a general distrust of suspects, believing that they lie to police 77.8% (SD = 20.0) of the time, it is not surprising that 51.8% also believe it would be easy for a suspect to make up a false alibi. This result may, in part, be due to the fact that suspects are most likely to offer family members (40.1%, SD = 24.5), significant others (34.0%, SD = 24.2) and friends (35.9%, SD = 25.7) as alibi witnesses, groups that Olson and Wells (2004) would classify as motivated familiar others. Ironically, law enforcement officers are most likely to perceive witnesses from these groups as lying about the alibi story during the investigation (48.1%, 53.3%, 45.1%, respectively; SDs = 26.3, 26.2, 27.4, respectively) or during their in court testimony (47.7%, 51.8%, 37.8%, respectively; SDs = 26.3, 26.2, 26.6, respectively). The non-motivated familiar other (i.e. acquaintance) and the non-motivated stranger are the most believable witnesses (25.8%, SD = 26.3, and 13.0%, SD = 22.1, lie to police; 18.3%, SD = 23.7, and 12.6%, SD = 22.1, lie in court), however, they are also the least commonly offered by suspects (23.4% and 13.2%, respectively, SDs = 25.5, 20.2, respectively).

To further investigate police perceptions of alibi witnesses, we asked respondents why a stranger might lie for a suspect. We were particularly interested in these responses because prior research has suggested that strangers are not motivated to lie and thus can be considered the most believable type of alibi witness (Olson & Wells, 2004). If law enforcement officers were able to generate realistic and probable reasons why someone might lie for a complete stranger, the assumption that strangers are *per se* non-motivated may be called into question by the data. The results indicate that there are several plausible reasons why strangers might lie: distrust of the police and the criminal justice system (34.2% of responses), fear or pressure from the suspect (28.9%), the promise of money, acceptance in a group or other type of reward (22.4%), or feeling bad for the suspect (14.5%).

Mistaken alibis

Respondents were asked whether they believe that a delay in time (10 minutes, 24 hours and 1 week) between the critical event (e.g. crime) and a suspect interview could affect the accuracy of a suspect's alibi story. When asked whether a suspect could be mistaken about where they were 10 minutes earlier, not surprisingly, 93.0% of respondents asserted that it was very or extremely *unlikely* that the suspect could be wrong. When asked about a 24-hour time frame, 56.1% continued to assert that mistakes were either very or extremely *unlikely*. And when we asked whether suspects could be mistaken about where they were and what they were doing 1 week earlier, 13% continued to assert that it was very or extremely *unlikely* that a mistake could be made. However some respondents (27.8%) believed that it was very or extremely *likely* that a suspect could be mistaken about their whereabouts. These results are interesting in light of responses to a question about why a suspect might change their initial alibi story: respondents believe that 81.4% (SD = 16.2) of suspects change their story because they were originally lying, as opposed to having been originally mistaken (19.1%, SD = 17.3).

We also asked respondents to provide reasons why a suspect might be mistaken about their alibi after a 10-minute delay between the time in question and the interview. Respondents ($N = 35$ responses) reported drug and/or alcohol use (48.6%), mental illness (28.6%), and trauma or stress (22.9%) as being potential reasons for making an error. With regards to why suspects might be mistaken after a 1-week delay ($N = 60$ responses), drug and alcohol use continued to be the most common response (28.3%), followed by: people generally have poor memories (26.7%), events that are not significant are not readily remembered (16.7%), busy individuals may have a more difficult time remembering a specific day (11.7%), questions of a general time frame are too difficult to recall (6.7%), and 10% of respondents responded with a personal statement about how poor their own memory can be. Some examples from the 24-hour delay question include: 'Memory is fallible. I don't remember where I was or what I was doing a week ago without checking a date book or my notebook'; 'People don't have the ability to recall exactly what they were doing at a certain time until they can associate it with a significant event'; and 'They are not familiar with or involved in the alleged incident. The stress of having to provide an alibi can often block the details of earlier experiences.'

Respondents were also asked, 'in cases where a suspect and the person verifying the alibi story are strangers, how likely is it that the stranger could be mistaken about their story? (1 = not at all likely, 10 = extremely likely).' The average response was 4.2 (SD = 1.8), with nobody selecting 10 on the scale. But when asked to give examples of why a stranger might be mistaken, respondents ($N = 50$) reported common and highly likely reasons: for example, the stranger was not paying attention or the event was not significant (36%), the stranger is not familiar with the suspect and therefore could be mistaken about the suspect's identity (30%), the stranger could be confusing the time in question (18%), and people make mistakes/ memory is fallible (16%).

Physical evidence

In general, previous research on alibi believability – including the responses from respondents in this survey – has shown that physical alibi evidence is more believable than person alibi evidence. However, we have no data on how often suspects in real cases provide leads to physical evidence in support of their alibi story. If physical evidence is uncommon, then there is an increased chance that a typical alibi story will not be believed. Unfortunately, the results of our survey reveal that suspects provide leads or references to physical alibi evidence in only 24.1% (SD = 21.8) of criminal cases.

We asked respondents to provide examples of physical evidence that suspects offer in criminal investigations and, for each example, to estimate how easy/difficult it would be for the suspect to fabricate that evidence (scale from 1 to 10, 1 = easy to fabricate, 10 = impossible to fabricate). Overall, respondents indicated that jail/incarceration records are the most difficult to fabricate evidence ($M = 10.0$, $SD = 0.00$), followed by video surveillance ($M = 8.6$, $SD = 1.4$), a time clock card or other evidence from the suspect's place of employment ($M = 6.8$, $SD = 1.2$), cell phone or land line records ($M = 6.1$, $SD = 2.5$), forms or applications ($M = 5.5$, $SD = 0.7$), receipts ($M = 5.2$, $SD = 2.7$), and photographs ($M = 3.0$, $SD = 0.0$). Using a slight modification of the alibi taxonomy, we categorized respondents' fabrication ratings into three groups (rather than two): easy to fabricate (scores of 1 – 3), moderate (scores of 4–7), and difficult to fabricate (scores of 8–10). The results and frequency of responses are presented in Table 1. There are three notable points about the results: First, the only category of physical evidence that contained no variability (with scores of 10) was if the suspect had been incarcerated at the time in question. Second, receipts, depending on the type and the details of the transaction (e.g. out of town receipt with name and signature vs ticket stub), were deemed highly variable in their ability to be fabricated. And third, although video surveillance evidence was almost uniformly rated as difficult to fabricate, several respondents noted that this type of evidence is extremely rare and that it is only difficult to fabricate if the suspect had no control over the video at any time.

Discussion

The purpose of our survey was to investigate both current law enforcement practice concerning the collection and investigation of alibi evidence and to determine what are law enforcement officers' opinions, beliefs, and experiences regarding alibis. Taken together, we see two dominant themes emerging from our data. First, is the issue of 'time.' Specifically, our respondents clearly understood that the sooner an alibi story can be investigated the greater the likelihood that the alibi story will be useful in determining whether the suspect was involved in the crime. Indeed, we saw evidence of this belief throughout the responses to our survey. For example, law enforcement officers endorsed the literature on autobiographical memory with their

Table 1. Types of evidence provided by suspects in criminal cases as a function of ability to fabricate that evidence (frequency of responses in parentheses).

	Ability to fabricate		
	Easy	Moderate	Difficult
Type of evidence	receipts (10)	receipts (10)	receipts (8)
	cell/phone records (1)	cell/phone records (5)	cell/phone records (3)
	photographs (2)	video (5)	video (24)
		work time card (4)	work time card (2)
		forms/applications (2)	jail (10)

understanding that memory fades with the passage of time (see for example, Ebbinghaus, 1885/1913; Wixted, 2004), and added that physical evidence is more likely to be distorted or tampered with – or simply disappear – as time passes. Moreover, our respondents also stated that a delay increases the likelihood that alibi witnesses could be pressured or influenced by the suspect or the suspect's associates to alter their stories.

As stated above, the passage of time appears to be a critical element in the overall believability of an alibi story. However, only a small number of our respondents (11%) indicated that the person who received the alibi statement should be the person to follow-up on the story. The conclusion we draw from this figure is that the procedures police currently endorse seem likely to increase the delay between the time a suspect offers their alibi story and when that alibi is investigated. Together, the implication of our results for law enforcement investigative practice is that alibi stories should be investigated as quickly as possible. In some circumstances, this would translate to patrol officers following up on an alibi story, in effect altering the practice described by many of our respondents. As a result, one recommendation that follows from our survey is that patrol officers receive more advanced training in investigative techniques.

Furthermore, we are aware of no mock jury studies that have examined the effects of delay in the investigation on the believability of alibi stories and thus these findings may contribute to future alibi believability research. In light of Olson and Charman's (in press) results showing that 30% of participants who provided alibi stories for the recent past were incorrect about their initial alibi story, and 42% were incorrect for alibis in the distant past, this line of research is timely and will be informative for law enforcement and criminal justice practitioners.

The second theme we identified is the inherent distrust of suspects that law enforcement officers hold, an issue that has been raised in prior research (see for example, Hartwig, Granhag, Strömwall, & Kronkvist, 2006 or Meissner & Kassin, 2002). Recall that 28% of our respondents believed that, when asked about their whereabouts 1 week earlier, it was very or extremely *likely* that a suspect could be mistaken. However, when those same respondents were asked why a suspect might change their initial alibi story, rather than restating that they could simply have been mistaken (an option only 19% endorsed), 81% asserted that if suspects change their story over time it is because they were originally lying. Clearly this overwhelming distrust puts innocent suspects who fall victim to the frailties of human memory in a tenuous position in the investigation (Brewer, 1988; Friedman, 2004; Skowronski et al., 1991; Thompson et al., 1996); a position, of course, that many of the DNA exonerees are well-acquainted with (see Innocence Project, 2010). The implication of these findings for suspects is that it is likely that the police officer in charge of their case will perceive that the suspect is lying about their alibi, making it a low priority for investigation, increasing the delay, and consequently increasing the probability that the alibi corroborator will misremember the time/event in question. Thus, the decision to investigate an alibi story quickly could increase the probative value of that evidence thus assisting (or shaping) the overall investigation.

There are of course limitations to the findings we present here. First, we have a rather small sample and as such it would be unwise to generalize our findings to any great extent. In addition, it is important to restate that the majority of our sample was senior level officers with investigative experience rather than 'on the ground' patrol officers. It would be interesting in future studies to see if the perceptions of our senior officers are mirrored in junior, patrol, officers and to examine whether perceptions of law enforcement are moderated by rural vs urban samples, and jurisdiction/country of residence. In addition, it is possible that the responses provided by law enforcement in this study were influenced by social desirability and that the individuals who finished the survey were somehow different than those who did not respond to the survey at all and those that completed only the demographic questions and were dropped from the remainder of the analyses. Thus, replication with a larger sample (covering the issues raised above) is encouraged.

To conclude, our law enforcement respondents provided some interesting information that should be valuable to the emerging alibi literature. In some cases, there appears to be a disconnect between respondents' beliefs, their investigative practice, and the empirical literature. While we recognize that we had a small sample, our respondents covered a large proportion of the United States and had significant experience with alibis, thus, we are fairly confident in the diversity of our responses. Of course, as we move towards a more comprehensive under-standing of alibi construction, investigation, and believability, we encourage researchers to pursue more research with the people who make decisions about whether to proceed with a criminal case against a suspect who has provided an alibi story.

References

Allison, M., & Brimacombe, C.A.E. (2010). Alibi believability: The effect of prior convictions and judicial instructions. *Journal of Applied Social Psychology, 40*, 1054–1084.

Brewer, W.F. (1988). Qualitative analysis of the recalls of randomly sampled autobiographical events. In M.M. Gruneberg, P.E. Morris, & R.N. Sykes (Eds.), *Practical aspects of memory: Current research and issues* (Vol. 1, pp. 263–268). Chichester: Wiley.

Burke, T.M., & Turtle, J.W. (2003). Alibi evidence in criminal investigations and trials: Psychological and legal factors. *The Canadian Journal of Police & Security Services, 1*, 286–294.

Burke, T.M., Turtle, J.W., & Olson, E.A. (2007). Alibis in criminal investigations. In M.P. Toglia, J.D. Read, D.F. Ross, & R.C.L. Lindsay (Eds.), *The Handbook of eyewitness psychology* vol. I: *memory for events* (pp. 157–174). Mahwah, NJ: Lawrence Erlbaum Associates.

Craig, J.D.R. (1996). The alibi exception to the right to silence. *Criminal Law Quarterly, 39*, 227–249.

Culhane, S.E., & Hosch, H.M. (2004). An alibi witness's influence on mock jurors' verdicts. *Journal of Applied Social Psychology, 34*, 1604–1616.

Dahl, L.C., Brimacombe, C.A.E., & Lindsay, D.S. (2009). Investigating investigators: How presentation order influences participant–investigators' interpretations of eyewitness identification and alibi evidence. *Law and Human Behavior, 33*, 368–380.

Ebbinghaus, H. (1885/1913). *Memory: A contribution to experimental psychology.* New York: Teachers College/Columbia University (Engl. ed.).

Epstein, D.M. (1964). Advance notice of alibi. *Journal of Criminal Law, Criminology, and Police Science, 55*, 29–38.

Friedman, W.J. (2004). Time in autobiographical memory. *Social Cognition, 22*, 605–621.

Hartwig, M., Granhag, P.A., Strömwall, L.A., & Kronkvist, O. (2006). Strategic use of evidence during police interviews: When training to detect deception. *Law and Human Behavior, 30*, 603–619.

Innocence Project (2010). Retrived from http://www.InnocenceProject.org (Accessed 30 June 2010).

McAllister, H.A., & Bregman, M.J. (1989). Juror underutilization of eyewitness nonidentifications: A test of the disconfirmed expectancy explanation. *Journal of Applied Social Psychology, 19*, 20–29.

Meissner, C.A., & Kassin, S.M. (2002). 'He's guilty!': Investigator bias in judgments of truth and deception. *Law and Human Behavior, 26*, 469–480.

Olson, E.A. (2002). *Where were you last night? Alibi believability and corroborating evidence: A new direction in psychology and law.* (Unpublished master's thesis). Iowa State University.

Olson, E.A., & Charman, S. (in press). 'But can you prove it?' Examining the quality of innocent suspects' alibis. *Psychology, Crime & Law.* doi:10.1080/1068316x.2010.505567.

Olson, E., & Wells, G. (2004). What makes a good alibi? A proposed taxonomy. *Law and Human Behavior, 28*, 157–176.

P. v Brown, 306 AD2d 12, 761 NYS2d 630 (1st Dept 2003).

Sargent, M.J., & Bradfield, A.L. (2004). Race and information processing in criminal trials: Does the defendant's race affect how the facts are evaluated? *Personality and Social Psychology Bulletin, 30*, 995–1008.

Skowronski, J.J., Betz, A.L., Thompson, C.P., & Shannon, L. (1991). Social memory in everyday life: Recall of self-events and other-events. *Journal of Personality and Social Psychology, 60*, 831–843.

Sommers, S.R., & Douglass, A.B. (2007). Context matters: Alibi strength varies according to evaluator perspective. *Legal and Criminological Psychology, 12*, 41–54.

Talarico, J.M., & Rubin, D.C. (2003). Confidence, not consistency, characterizes flashbulb memories. *Psychological Science, 14*, 455–461.

Thompson, C.P., Skowronski, J.J., Larsen, S.F., & Betz, A. (1996). *Autobiographical memory: Remembering what and remembering when.* Hillsdale, NJ: Lawrence Erlbaum.

Wixted, J. (2004). The psychology and neuroscience of forgetting. *Annual Review of Psychology, 55*, 235–269.

Appendix 1 (response options in parentheses)

General alibi questions

(1) Have you ever received specific training on how to interview alibi witnesses? (yes/no)
(2) In your experience as a police officer, how many times has a suspect provided you with an alibi story? (open)
(3) In cases involving a person's whereabouts at the time of the crime, what percentage of the time do suspects give spontaneous alibi statements to police? (open)
(4) In your opinion, what is the most solid (believable) alibi story that someone can give? (open)

Investigation: procedures

(5) Thinking only of patrol officers, what percentage of the time do they follow-up on a suspect's alibi story? (open)
(6) Thinking only of detectives, what percentage of the time do they follow-up on a suspect's alibi story? (open)
(7) In serious crimes, a suspect's alibi is thoroughly investigated before a warrant is prepared or an arrest made. (always/often/sometimes/rarely/never/not sure)
(8) When police are talking with a suspect, what percentage of the time do they ask the suspect where they on a specific day and time? For example, 'Where were you on Tuesday, April 4th between 2:00 and 2:30 pm?' (open)
(9) When police talk to a suspect, what percentage of the time do they ask the suspect where they were during a broad time frame? For example, 'Where were you on Tuesday, April 4th?' (open)

Investigation: responsibility

(10) In your opinion, whose responsibility is it to investigate a suspect's alibi story? (open)
(11) What percentage of the time do the following groups of people investigate alibi statements:
(a) Police, (b) Prosecutors, (c) Public defenders, (d) Private defense attorneys (open)
(12) If a suspect provided an alibi statement and the police did not investigate that statement, would you consider it to be substandard police investigative practice? (yes/no/not sure)
(13) If a suspect provided an alibi statement and the police did not investigate that statement, would you consider it to be police misconduct? (yes/no/not sure)
(14) If a suspect provided an alibi statement and the prosecutor did not investigate that statement, would you consider it to be prosecutorial misconduct? (yes/no/not sure)
(15) If a suspect provided an alibi statement and their defense attorney did not investigate that statement, would you consider it to be substandard defense lawyering? (yes/no/not sure)

Alibi frequency and lying

(16) What percentage of the time do suspects lie when they are interviewed by police? (open)
(17) When suspects offer an alibi statement, what percentage of the time do they offer people from the following groups to support their story? (open)
(a) Family members, (b) Significant other, (c) Friends, (d) Acquaintances, (e) Strangers
(18) For each of the following groups, what percentages of people who come forward as an alibi witness for a suspect are lying? (open)
(a) Family members, (b) Significant other, (c) Friends, (d) Acquaintances, (e) Strangers
(19) In your opinion, why would a stranger lie for a suspect and tell a false alibi story to the police? (open)

Mistaken alibis

(20) If a suspect was asked where they were 10 minutes earlier, how likely is it that the suspect could be mistaken about their alibi story? (scale 1–10, not sure; 1 = not at all likely, 10 = extremely likely)
(21) From the previous question, please provide a reason why a suspect might be mistaken if they were asked about where they were 10 minutes earlier. (open)
(22) If a suspect was asked where they were 24 hours earlier, how likely is it that the suspect could be mistaken about their alibi story? (scale 1–10, not sure; 1 = not at all likely, 10 = extremely likely)
(23) If a suspect was asked where they were exactly 1 week earlier, how likely is it that they could be mistaken about their alibi story? (scale 1–10, not sure; 1 = not at all likely, 10 = extremely likely)
(24) From the previous question, please provide a reason why a suspect could be mistaken if they were asked about where they were 1 week earlier. (open)
(25) When a suspect changes their initial alibi story, what percentage changes their story because they were:
(a) originally lying? (open);
(b) originally mistaken? (open)

(26) In cases where a suspect and the person verifying the alibi story are strangers (e.g. store clerk), how likely is it that the stranger could be mistaken about their story? (scale 1–10, not sure; 1 = not at all likely, 10 = extremely likely)

(27) From the previous question, why might a stranger be mistaken about the alibi story? (open)

Physical evidence

(28) What percentage of the time do suspects provide leads or references to physical evidence in support of their alibi? (open)

(29) From the previous question, what kinds of physical evidence do suspects provide? For each example you list, please indicate how difficult you believe it would be to fabricate each type of evidence on a scale from 1 to 10 (1 = easy to fabricate, 10 = impossible to fabricate). (open)

Alibi example

(30) Please describe (in as much detail as you can) a suspect's alibi story that you believed to be true. This can be a story that you believed (on the spot) without further investigation or one that was later verified before you accepted the story. (open)

Do jurors get what they expect? Traditional versus alternative forms of children's testimony

Bradley D. McAuliff[a] and Margaret Bull Kovera[b]

[a]Department of Psychology, California State University, Northridge, USA; [b]John Jay College of Criminal Justice, City University New York, USA

This study examined prospective jurors' expectancies for the verbal and nonverbal behavior of a child testifying in a sexual abuse case. Community members ($N = 261$) reporting for jury duty completed a survey in which they described their expectancies for how a child alleging sexual abuse would appear when testifying and their beliefs about discerning children's truthfulness, testimony stress, and fairness to trial parties. Within this survey, we varied the child's age (5, 10, or 15 years old), type of abuse alleged (vaginal fondling or penetration), and whether the abuse actually occurred (yes, no) between participants across five different testimony conditions (traditional live in-court, support person present, closed-circuit television, preparation, and videotape) within each participant. Participants expected a child providing traditional testimony to be more nervous, tearful, and fidgety; less confident, cooperative, and fluent; and to maintain less eye contact and provide shorter responses than when the child provided alternative forms of testimony. Participants believed it was easiest to determine a child's truthfulness and fairest to the defendant when the child testified live in court, but that this form of testimony was the most stressful and unfair to the child. Expectancies and beliefs differed within the alternative forms of testimony as well. Negative evaluations of children's alternative testimony may be the result of expectancy violation; namely, jurors expect differences in children's verbal and nonverbal behavior as a result of accommodation, but those differences actually do not occur.

Introduction

Testifying in court can be stressful for any witness, particularly for child victims of physical or sexual abuse (Goodman et al., 1992; Quas et al., 2005). Several features of traditional trial proceedings (exposure to unfamiliar personnel and procedures, multiple interviews containing complex vocabulary, describing intimate abuse details in open court, confronting the accused) may make children reluctant to testify (Goodman et al., 1992; Sas, 1991) and may decrease the accuracy of their testimony (Goodman et al., 1998; Saywitz & Nathanson, 1993). If children are unwilling to testify about abuse or are inaccurate when doing so, it becomes increasingly difficult to prevent these crimes and the drastic toll they exact on children's physical and mental health.

Evidentiary and procedural innovations for children

Various evidentiary and procedural innovations have been introduced over the past two decades to help enable child victims to testify in child abuse proceedings (Hall & Sales, 2008; McAuliff & Kovera, 2002; Sandler, 2006). At the federal level, for example, the Victims of Child Abuse Act of 1990 (§3266) amended the Federal Rules of Criminal Procedure, extending special accommodations to children such as allowing the presence of a support person during the child's testimony or closing the courtroom (Whitcomb, 1992). Most state legislatures also have enacted statutes permitting the use of innovative procedures, such as videotape or closed-circuit television (CCTV) testimony, in trials involving alleged child abuse victims. These modifications constitute a broad spectrum of alternatives to traditional testimony that are designed to reduce the stress associated with appearing in court and to increase the accuracy of children's testimony.

Despite the widespread availability of innovations, we know little about jurors' views regarding the use of such procedures in child abuse cases. Instead previous research has focused on the frequency with which courts have implemented innovative procedures (Hafemeister, 1996; Sigler, Crowley, & Johnson, 1990) and their efficacy (Cashmore, 1992; Davies & Noon, 1991; Davies, Wilson, Mitchell, & Milsom, 1995; Murray, 1995; Plotnikoff & Woolfson, 2000; Saywitz, Synder, & Nathanson, 1999). Social scientists have not entirely overlooked the issue of how alternative testimony procedures influence jurors' perceptions in cases involving children. Early research examining videotape (Swim, Borgida, & McCoy, 1993), CCTV (Lindsay, Ross, Lea, & Carr, 1995; Ross et al., 1994) and hearsay testimony (Golding, Sanchez, & Sego, 1997) revealed that mock jurors' perceptions of defendants and children generally do not vary as a function of testimony mode. However, these studies relied exclusively on college student samples and held child demeanor and testimony constant across the various testimony conditions. Consequently, we do not know whether the results generalize to actual jurors or whether accommodations alter children's behavior and testimony in ways that in turn influence jurors' perceptions and decisions.

One experiment improved upon these limitations by including jury-eligible community members and by randomly assigning children to testify either live in court or outside the courtroom via CCTV (Goodman et al., 1998). Children described an earlier play session in which an unfamiliar male confederate had them place stickers on their clothing (defendant innocent condition) or exposed body parts (defendant guilty condition). There was no evidence that the use of CCTV biased mock jurors against the defendant. More striking, however, were the results pertaining to mock jurors' impressions of children who testified live or via CCTV (reported in Tobey, Goodman, Batterman-Faunce, Orcutt, & Sachsenmaier, 1995). They perceived CCTV testifiers to be less believable, less accurate in recalling the event, more likely to have made up the story, less likely to have based their testimony on fact than fiction, less attractive, less intelligent, less confident, and less stressed than children who testified live in court. Similar effects emerged in a second study in which mock jurors rated children who testified via CCTV as being less detailed, less confident, and less forthcoming than children who testified live (Landström & Granhag, 2010). That study also included a videotaped testimony condition and those children were seen as more defensive and less confident, involved, thoughtful, straightforward, natural, eloquent, pleasant, and forthcoming than children testifying live.

These experiments illustrate a perplexing dilemma that faces courts and professionals who contemplate the use of alternative testimony procedures with children. Despite the ability of certain accommodations to reduce children's stress and increase their accuracy, mock jurors tend to evaluate accommodated children more negatively on a variety of dimensions. Why might this occur? Some researchers have suggested that a vividness effect could be at play (Landström & Granhag, 2010). According to the vividness effect, observers pay more attention to, evaluate more positively, and better remember testimony that is 'emotionally interesting, concrete, and imagery provoking, and proximate in a sensory, temporal, or spatial way' than testimony that lacks these features (Nisbett & Ross, 1980, p. 45). Essentially jurors respond more favorably to live testimony because it is more vivid in many ways than videotape or CCTV testimony broadcast on television monitors. Whereas the medium of testimony is central to the vividness effect explanation, we were interested in examining a second possibility that focuses more on children's behavior while testifying. Perhaps accommodating children changes their verbal and/or nonverbal behavior in ways that negatively affect jurors' perceptions.

To our knowledge, only one experiment has systematically examined this issue. Kovera, Gresham, Borgida, Gray, and Regan (1997) surveyed attorneys to determine what typical behaviors are exhibited by prepared versus unprepared child witnesses. They used attorneys' responses to develop a trial simulation in which an actress portrayed the child witness as either prepared (the child made eye contact, sat still, and responded confidently) or unprepared (the child looked down, fidgeted, and responded hesitantly). When mock jurors were reminded (via effective expert testimony) that children who are abused may be confused and uncertain, they were more likely to convict the defendant when the child appeared unprepared versus prepared. No such differences emerged when mock jurors did not receive expert testimony.

Based on the existing empirical evidence that (1) mock jurors evaluate children more negatively when courts accommodate children and (2) certain accommodations may alter children's testimony behavior, we wanted to explore one theoretical explanation that might account for these outcomes: expectancy violation.

Expectancy violation theory

Expectancy violation theory (EVT; Burgoon & Hale, 1988) posits that people approach social interactions expecting others to engage in certain verbal and nonverbal behaviors. Expectancies are based largely on social norms and past experience, but they also include the known idiosyncrasies of others. In essence, people expect behaviors that they consider to be typical and feasible for a particular setting, purpose, and set of participants. Expectancy violations attract attention and result in an interpretation/evaluation process in which people assess the meaning of the expectancy violation, assign it a positive or negative valence, and react accordingly. EVT predicts that people will react more favorably to positive expectancy violations than they will to negative expectancy violations. Indeed, findings from studies by Burgoon and her colleagues have supported this prediction (Burgoon, 1993; Burgoon & Hale, 1988; Burgoon & LePoire, 1993; Burgoon & Walther, 1990).

Expectancy violations can affect people's attitudes and decision-making processes in legal settings as well (Ask & Landström, 2010; Feldman & Chesley, 1984; Salekin, Ogloff, McFarland, & Rogers, 1995). Yet only one published study to date has directly examined the effects on mock jurors' perceptions of expectancy violations committed by a child witness. In that study, Schmidt and Brigham (1996) hypothesized that participants would react unfavorably when a child used a communication style that violated age-appropriate stereotypes. College students viewed a child witness of various ages (5, 10, or 15 years old) who engaged in a powerful or powerless communication style while testifying. The child's powerful communication style was characterized by confident responses, direct eye contact, and a lack of hesitancy when answering questions. In contrast, children displaying the powerless communication style were more fidgety, maintained less eye contact, and used more nonfluencies and hesitations. Mock jurors rated the powerless 15-year-old witness as the least truthful and least intelligent of all the child witnesses.

Building on this preliminary evidence, we explored the role of EVT in explaining why mock jurors evaluated children more negatively when they provided alternative forms of testimony. Unlike Schmidt and Brigham, who assumed that mock jurors hold certain expectancies for children's testimony behavior (confidence, eye contact, fluency), we assessed the exact nature of jurors' actual expectancies for a child's verbal and nonverbal testimony behavior. We reasoned that if accommodations serve their intended purpose (i.e., reducing stress and increasing accuracy), they should result in a child who is less nervous, fidgety, or tearful and more confident, cooperative, or fluent than when accommodations are not used. Eventhough this outcome certainly is desirable from the child's standpoint, it may violate jurors' expectancies and consequently lead to more negative evaluations. For example, jurors may expect child victims to be somewhat nervous, fidgety, tearful, unconfident, uncooperative, and not very fluent when testifying at trial. Viewing an accommodated child who violates these expectancies may create feelings of doubt or skepticism. Jurors may misattribute the more relaxed and confident demeanor of the accommodated child to other sources, such as coaching from a parent or suggestive and leading questioning from a law enforcement officer. In this sense, an accommodated child's behavior that exceeds jurors' expectancies could lead to negative consequences for the child because jurors expect one thing and get another.

A second possibility also exists. Even though jurors may expect a child providing traditional testimony to be nervous, tearful, unconfident, and not very fluent, they may modify their expectancies based on the knowledge that a particular child was accommodated before (preparation) or during trial (support person, CCTV). They may expect the child to be calm, tearless, confident, and fluent as a result of the accommodation. If true, then jurors' expectancies could be violated in the opposite direction described above for a child who remains nervous, tearful, unconfident, and lacks fluency despite accommodation. Experiments have documented the ability of certain accommodations to reduce stress at statistically significant levels compared to traditional testimony; however, those comparisons were relative in nature and children's stress levels remained fairly high in both conditions (Goodman et al., 1998;

Landström & Granhag, 2010). Should a similar outcome occur in actual cases, then children using accommodations may be disadvantaged compared to children who do not. Classic attribution theory (Heider, 1958; Kelley, 1972) asserts that people consider a variety of factors (or causes) when making attributions about others based on their behavior. People are less likely to make dispositional inferences about others' behavior when other plausible explanations for the observed behavior exist. Whereas jurors who view traditional testimony may apply the discounting principle and attribute the child's stress or impaired testimony performance to situational factors such as testifying in court or having to face the defendant, it is more difficult for jurors to do so when the child is accommodated because accommodations can attenuate (preparation or support) or eliminate (CCTV) these situational factors. Once stripped of plausible situational explanations, jurors may instead make dispositional inferences about the child's behavior; one possible inference is that the child is lying.

Jurors' beliefs about alternative testimony procedures

We also wanted to learn prospective jurors' beliefs about how alternative testimony procedures might affect different participants in the trial process. Specifically, we wondered whether jurors believed that the different forms of testimony would influence (1) their ability to discern the child's truthfulness, (2) the amount of stress experienced by the child, and (3) the fairness to the child and defendant. Scant research has examined whether mock jurors' ability to discern children's truthfulness varies as a function of testimony format. However, adults in a study by Landström and Granhag (2010) viewed children's live, videotaped, or CCTV statements about an event that was either experienced or imagined. No significant differences emerged between observers' rates of accuracy across the three conditions. These null effects were consistent with earlier work (Orcutt et al., 2001), in which jurors' ability to detect children's deception did not vary as a function of viewing live or CCTV testimony.

With respect to the ability of accommodations to reduce children's stress, one survey found that prosecuting attorneys viewed preparation and the presence of a support person in court as 'particularly useful' whereas they viewed videotaped and CCTV testimony as 'useful' (Goodman, Quas, Bulkley, & Shapiro, 1999). Ninety percent of judges responding to another survey believed that allowing a child to testify on an adult's lap effectively minimized the child's trauma compared to 83% and 79% who felt the same about the use of videotape and CCTV, respectively (Hafemeister, 1996). Victim witness assistants share attorneys' and judges' optimism for the ability of support person use to reduce children's stress, particularly when the support person accompanies the child to trial and provides pretrial preparation (McAuliff, Nicholson, Amarilio, & Ravanshenas, in press). Quasi-experimental work on children in actual trials who provided traditional versus prepared (Sas, 1991, 1993), videotaped (Davies et al., 1995), or CCTV testimony (Cashmore, 1992; Davies & Noon, 1988; Murray, 1995) showed that the vast majority of legal professionals believed the innovations effectively reduced children's stress. Finally, experiments in which researchers randomly assigned children to testimony conditions have found that mock jurors rated children testifying via CCTV as being less stressed than children testifying in open court (Goodman et al., 1998) and that children's self-reports of stress while providing videotaped testimony were lower than children testifying live or via CCTV (Landström & Granhag, 2010).

Whether traditional or innovative testimony is considered 'fair' to children and defendants depends in part on the operational definition of fairness. When participants rate fairness directly, they report that the use of videotape (Swim et al., 1993) and CCTV (Lindsay et al., 1995) is fair to the defendant. Victim witness assistants reported that the presence of a support person at trial probably does not prejudice jurors against a defendant (McAuliff et al., in press). Other studies have measured fairness more indirectly by examining whether verdicts or perceptions of either party differ as a function of testimony format. Few differences were present in these studies either (Eaton, Ball, & O'Callaghan, 2001; Lindsay et al., 1995; Ross et al., 1994; Swim et al., 1993) and when differences did emerge, they tended to favor defendants. For example, Swim et al. (1999) found that mock jurors were less likely to convict a defendant when the alleged child victim provided videotaped (30%) versus live in court (48%) testimony. Most recently, Eaton et al. (2001) compared children's live, videotaped, and CCTV testimony and found that mock jurors rendered guilty verdicts more often when the child testified live versus via videotape or CCTV. Unlike these experiments, where children's testimony and demeanor was held constant across testimony conditions, Goodman et al. (1998) randomly assigned children to testify live or via CCTV and did not find any evidence that the use of CCTV biased mock jurors against the defendant.

In sum, viewing children's traditional versus innovative forms of testimony appears to have little if any effect on mock jurors' ability to detect children's truthfulness and their perceptions of fairness to children and defendants; however, mock jurors and various legal professionals do believe that innovative procedures reduce children's stress compared to traditional testimony.

Overview

We designed the present study to address three primary research questions. First, what types of verbal and nonverbal behavior do prospective jurors expect children to exhibit when testifying? Second, do these expectancies vary as a function of the means by which children provide testimony? And third, do prospective jurors' beliefs about discerning children's truthfulness, children's stress, and fairness to children and defendants vary across different forms of testimony? To answer these questions, we constructed a survey in which we manipulated several variables to assess their potential impact on prospective jurors' expectancies and beliefs.

Method

Participants

Two hundred and sixty-one US citizens (*M* age = 42 years) reporting for jury duty in South Florida volunteered to participate in a study about juror decision making. Most participants were White (69%), married (54%), had children (62%) and reported a gross family income of $60 000 or less (66%). Twenty-seven percent of participants indicated their highest level of educational achievement was some high school or a high school diploma and 57% indicated their highest level of education was some college or a college degree. Most jurors (72%) had not served on a civil or criminal jury before. An approximately equal number of men and women participated in exchange for a meal voucher at a restaurant located in the courthouse complex ($ns = 122$ and 137, respectively; two participants did not identify their sex).

Stimulus materials

Survey

Each survey included a description of a female child who claimed to have been sexually abused. The description of the child varied on three dimensions: the child's age, the type of abuse alleged, and whether the alleged abuse actually occurred. Specifically, the survey described the child as 5, 10, or 15 years old. Half of the descriptions indicated that she claimed that the defendant had fondled her; the other half stated that she alleged the defendant had vaginally penetrated her. Orthogonal to these manipulations, we also varied whether participants were informed that the alleged abuse did or did not actually occur. We instructed participants to consider how a child witness fitting this description would typically behave if he or she testified in five different testimony conditions: traditional live in-court testimony, support person present during testimony, prepared testimony, videotaped testimony, or CCTV testimony.

We introduced each of the five testimony conditions by providing a brief paragraph that described each procedure and how it is used at trial. The paragraph describing the procedure for traditional live in-court testimony was as follows:

> In this procedure, all persons involved in the trial remain in the same courtroom. The child is sworn in under oath and sits alone in the witness stand (usually at the front of the courtroom) in full view of the defendant, judge, attorneys, and jury. The child is questioned directly by the prosecuting attorney and then cross-examined by the defendant's attorney. The defendant, judge, attorneys, and jury view the child face-to-face during his or her live testimony.

We modified this basic description to suit each of the four alternative testimony conditions. See Table 1 for these complete descriptions.

Dependent measures

Participants provided their expectancies for the child's verbal and nonverbal behavior in the different testimony conditions using a series of relevant seven-point bipolar adjective pairs. We averaged across ratings for the different adjective pairs to form five composite variables of how nervous, tearful, confident, rehearsed, and fidgety participants expected the child to appear when testifying and one for how fluent the child's speech would be. The adjective pairs used for these six scales and their final reliability coefficients appear in Table 2. We also used three single adjective pairs to measure expectancies for the child's cooperativeness, level of eye contact, and response length in the different testimony conditions.

Next participants used a series of four seven-point, Likert-type scales to indicate their beliefs about their ability to determine the child's truthfulness, the stressfulness

Table 1. Descriptions of alternative testimony conditions provided to participants.

Alternative Testimony Condition	Description
Live In-Court Testimony with Support Person Present	In this procedure, all persons involved in the trial remain in the same courtroom. The child is sworn in under oath and testifies from the witness stand (usually at the front of the courtroom) in full view of the defendant, judge, attorneys, and jury. However, unlike traditional live, in-court testimony where the child sits alone in the witness stand, a person (e.g. a family member or someone appointed by the court) is seated next to the child to provide emotional support while the child testifies. The child is questioned directly by the prosecuting attorney and then cross-examined by the defendant's attorney. The defendant, judge, attorneys, and jury view the child face-to-face during his or her live testimony.
Closed-Circuit Television (CCTV) Testimony	In this procedure, the child is sworn in under oath and sits in a room outside the courtroom. The prosecuting and defense attorneys, who are also present in the outside room, question and cross-examine the child just as they would if the child were testifying in the courtroom. A live simulcast of this process is transmitted to the defendant, judge, jury and others who remain in the courtroom. These individuals view and hear the child's testimony on a video monitor screen, similar to a television. Because the child remains in a room outside the courtroom, the defendant, judge, and jury do not view the child face-to-face during his or her live testimony.
Live In-Court Testimony with Preparation	In this procedure, before the trial, the child participates in special procedures designed to prepare the child for his or her upcoming court appearance. These procedures can include a tour of the courtroom, a meeting with the judge and attorneys in the case, and an opportunity for the child to ask any questions he or she has about testifying in court. When the child later testifies at trial, all involved persons remain in the same courtroom. The child is sworn in under oath and sits alone in the witness stand (usually at the front of the courtroom) in full view of the defendant, judge, attorneys, and jury. The child is questioned directly by the prosecuting attorney and then cross-examined by the defendant's attorney. The defendant, judge, attorneys, and jury view the child face-to-face during his or her live testimony.
Videotape Testimony	Videotape testimony can take one of several forms when used in court. One of the most common forms is the videotaped deposition. In this procedure, the child is sworn in under oath and interviewed in a room outside of the courtroom before the actual trial begins. The defendant and both attorneys are present in the room with the child and other observers such as the judge also may also be present. The child is questioned and cross-examined by the attorneys just as he or she would be when testifying in court, however this process is videotaped. Later at trial, the child's videotape testimony may be played to replace the child's live, in-court testimony. All persons present during the child's original testimony view the child face-to-face; however, at trial jurors view and hear the child's videotape testimony on a video monitor screen, similar to a television.

Table 2. Adjective pairs and reliability coefficients for composite variables used to rate participants' expectancies for children's testimony behavior.

Composite variable	Cronbach's alpha	Adjective pairs
Nervous	0.86	
		Calm/Nervous
		Relaxed/Anxious
		Uncomfortable/Comfortable (R)
Tearful	0.86	
		Happy/Sad
		Smile/Frown
		Tearful/Tearless (R)
Confident	0.80	
		Confident/Intimidated (R)
		Fearless/Fearful (R)
		Timid/Brave
Rehearsed	0.91	
		Coached/Natural (R)
		Rehearsed/Spontaneous (R)
Fidgety	0.78	
		Fidgety/Motionless
		Still/Restless (R)
Fluent speech	0.81	
		Hesitant/Fluent
		Rapid/Slow speech rate (R)
		Stuttering/Steady speech

Note: adjective pairs followed by (R) were reverse scored for inclusion in composite variables.

of the child's testimony, and the fairness to the child and defendant in each of the five testimony conditions (1 = Not at all, 4 = Neutral, 7 = Extremely).

Prospective jurors concluded their participation by providing demographic information about their gender, age, jury eligibility, racial/ethnic identity, history of jury service, and previous involvement in legal proceedings (civil or criminal, plaintiff or defendant).

Procedure

Upon their arrival at the courthouse, the Chief Administrative Judge welcomed community members and provided a brief overview of what jury service would entail. At the conclusion of the orientation, the experimenter made an announcement inviting prospective jurors to participate in a study about juror decision making. Those who wished to participate reported to a lounge adjacent to the jury assembly room. After providing informed consent, participants received the stimulus and dependent measures. They did not confer with one another at any point during the study. After completing the study, participants were debriefed, given the opportunity to ask questions, and then offered the meal voucher as a token of appreciation for contributing to the research.

Design

Our study consisted of a 3 (Child Age: 5, 10, or 15 years old) × 2 (Abuse Type: fondling or penetration) × 2 (Allegation Veracity: true or false) × 5 (Testimony Condition: live, support person, CCTV, preparation, or videotape) mixed-factorial design. Child Age, Abuse Type, and Allegation Veracity were between-participants manipulations and Testimony Condition was a within-participants manipulation. We randomly assigned participants to the conditions while attempting to balance the number of men and women in each condition. We presented the testimony conditions to participants in five different orders. Each testimony condition appeared in one of five possible positions across the different presentation orders.

Results

Overall data analytic strategy and preliminary findings

We analyzed the data using a series of Child Age × Abuse Type × Allegation Veracity × Testimony Condition four-way mixed-model ANOVAs. Tukey's HSD tests were used for all follow-up comparisons. We only report the main effects that emerged as a function of our Testimony Condition manipulation because our primary research questions focused on whether prospective jurors' expectancies and beliefs about children's behavior vary across different forms of testimony. None of these main effects were qualified by significant interactions with any of the other manipulated variables except for the tearful, testimony stressfulness, and fairness to child dependent measures (see footnotes 1, 2, and 3).

A significant main effect of Testimony Condition emerged on all nine of the dependent measures of jurors' expectancies for children's testimony behavior (see Table 3 for all F-tests and means) and all four of the dependent measures of jurors' beliefs about truth determination, testimony stressfulness, and fairness to trial parties (see Table 4 for all F-tests and means). Next we describe the follow-up comparisons for the Testimony Condition main effect on each dependent measure.

Jurors' expectancies for children's testimony behavior

Nervous

Compared to all other conditions, participants expected the child to be the most nervous when providing traditional live in-court testimony and the least nervous when using a support person or CCTV. These latter two means were not significantly different from one another, but both were lower than participants' expectancies for the child's nervousness in the prepared testimony condition. Participants expected the videotaped child to be less nervous than the traditional testifier, but no other differences involving videotape testimony were statistically significant.

Tearful[1]

Participants expected the traditional testifier to be the most tearful compared to all other conditions and the least tearful when testifying with a support person or via CCTV. Expectancies for the child's prepared and videotaped testimony fell between these two extremes but did not significantly differ from one another. The ratings of

Table 3. Means and repeated-measure effects of testimony condition on participants' expectancies for children's testimony behavior.

Dependent measure	Means (SD)					Repeated-measures effects of testimony condition			
	Live	Support person	CCTV	Preparation	Videotape	F	d.f.	p	η_p^2
Nervous	5.75[a] (1.14)	4.60[b] (1.51)	4.58[b] (1.50)	5.12[c] (1.34)	4.85[b, c] (1.49)	46.29	4, 988	0.0001	0.16
Tearful	5.75[a] (1.14)	4.68[b, c] (1.23)	4.62[c] (1.22)	5.00[d] (1.18)	4.85[b, d] (1.18)	70.68	4, 988	0.0001	0.22
Confident	1.83[a] (1.26)	2.72[b] (1.36)	2.71[b] (1.31)	2.32[c] (1.30)	2.43[c] (1.29)	33.64	4, 980	0.0001	0.12
Rehearsed	4.36 (1.52)	4.55[a] (1.45)	4.23[b] (1.45)	4.49[a, c] (1.47)	4.32[b, c] (1.44)	4.81	4, 972	0.001	0.02
Cooperative	4.75[a] (1.59)	5.12[b] (1.43)	5.05[b] (1.47)	5.08[b] (1.40)	5.03[b] (1.45)	4.54	4, 988	0.001	0.02
Fidgety	5.13[b] (1.40)	4.55[b] (1.37)	4.67[b] (1.28)	4.78[b] (1.40)	4.66[b] (1.47)	11.55	4, 980	0.0001	0.05
Eye contact	2.84[a] (1.70)	3.38[b] (1.77)	3.47[b] (1.79)	3.29[b] (1.78)	3.31[b] (1.80)	7.30	4, 972	0.0001	0.03
Fluent speech	2.92[a] (1.27)	3.72[b] (1.28)	3.73[b] (1.30)	3.52[b] (1.27)	3.65[b] (1.36)	31.10	4, 984	0.0001	0.11
Response length	2.70[a] (1.52)	3.39[b] (1.61)	3.41[b] (1.59)	3.30[b] (1.63)	3.35[b] (1.62)	14.02	4, 984	0.0001	0.05

Notes: means sharing unique superscripts within each row were statistically significant at $p < 0.05$. Nervous, tearful, confident, rehearsed, fidgety, and fluent speech were all seven-point composite variables derived from adjective pairs described in Table 2. Eye contact, cooperative, and response length were single-item adjective pairs. Larger values correspond with higher levels of each respective dependent measure.

Table 4. Means and repeated-measures effects of testimony condition on participants' beliefs about determining children's truthfulness, testimony stressfulness, and fairness to trial parties.

Dependent measure	Means (SD)					Repeated-measures effects of testimony condition			
	Live	Support person	CCTV	Preparation	Videotape	F	d.f.	p	η_p^2
Ability to determine child's truthfulness	5.75[a] (1.14)	4.60[b] (1.51)	4.58[b] (1.50)	5.12[c] (1.34)	4.85[b, c] (1.49)	46.29	4, 988	0.0001	0.16
Testimony stressfulness	6.05[a] (1.28)	4.80[b] (1.70)	4.57[b] (1.68)	5.52[c] (1.49)	4.87[b, c] (1.65)	53.16	4, 976	0.0001	0.18
Fairness to child	3.77[a] (1.78)	4.92[b] (1.57)	5.03[b] (1.56)	4.24[c] (1.76)	5.08[b, d] (1.44)	42.63	4, 972	0.0001	0.15
Fairness to defendant	4.94[a] (1.57)	4.75 (1.58)	4.87 (1.50)	4.63[b] (1.57)	4.64[b] (1.54)	2.97	4, 964	0.02	0.01

Notes: means sharing unique superscripts within each row were statistically significant at $p < 0.05$. 1 = Not at all, 4 = Neutral, 7 = Extremely.

the child's expected tearfulness in the support person and videotape conditions were not statistically different.

Confident

Participants expected the child testifying with a support person or via CCTV to be the most confident, followed by the prepared and videotaped child. Expectancies for the child's confidence in the traditional live in-court condition were the lowest and significantly different from all four forms of alternative testimony.

Rehearsed

Participants expected the child to appear the most rehearsed in the support person and preparation conditions and the least rehearsed in the CCTV condition. They expected the videotaped child to appear less rehearsed than the supported child, but no different than the prepared or CCTV child. Expectancies for how rehearsed a traditional testifier would appear did not differ from any of the alternative testimony conditions.

Cooperative, fidgety, eye contact, fluent speech, and response length

The pattern of effects was the same across all five dependent measures: participants expected the traditional testifier to be less cooperative, more fidgety, maintain less eye contact, exhibit less fluent speech, and provide shorter responses than when the child testified using a support person, CCTV, preparation, or videotape. None of the differences between any of the four alternative testimony conditions were statistically significant.

Jurors' beliefs about truth determination, testimony stressfulness, and fairness to trial parties

Truth determination and testimony stressfulness[2]

Participants believed that they were best able to determine whether traditional testifiers were telling the truth, followed by prepared children, and the least able to do so when children testified with a support person present or via CCTV. Participants' beliefs about their ability to discern the truthfulness of the child's videotape testimony differed only from the live in-court testimony condition. They also believed it was most stressful for children to provide traditional testimony, followed by prepared testimony, and that support person and CCTV testimony were the least stressful. Participants believed children's videotape testimony was less stressful than traditional testimony; no other differences involving videotape testimony were statistically significant.

Fairness to child[3] and defendant

With respect to the child, participants believed that live in-court testimony was the least fair and that support person, CCTV, and videotape testimony were the most fair. Fairness ratings for the child in the preparation condition fell between these two sets of means and differed from all four conditions at a statistically significant level. In contrast, participants indicated that traditional live in-court testimony was fairer to the defendant than children's prepared or videotaped testimony. No other differences were statistically significant.

Discussion

We began by considering two EVT-based explanations for why mock jurors evaluate child witnesses more negatively when courts accommodate children. The first explanation stated that a child's testimony may exceed mock jurors' expectancies causing them to be more skeptical because they expect a child victim to be nervous, but accommodations reduce or eliminate this behavior. The second explanation stated that perhaps mock jurors overestimate the calming effects that accommodations have on children and their testimony. If accommodated children remain nervous, they may violate mock jurors' expectancies and be viewed negatively as a result. In fact, this second outcome might be even more detrimental than the first because accommodations may attenuate or eliminate one potential explanation for children's expectancy violating behavior, namely that the child is testifying live in court, which can be an extremely stressful experience for any witness.

Jurors' expectancies for children's testimony behavior

To shed light on these potential explanations, we began by measuring what expectancies prospective jurors hold for children's verbal and nonverbal behavior when providing different forms of testimony. Jurors' expectancies do in fact vary as a function of children's testimony condition. In general, participants in our study expected a child providing traditional live in-court testimony to be more nervous, tearful, and fidgety, and less confident and cooperative than a child providing alternative forms of testimony. They also expected the child to maintain less eye contact, to be less fluent, and to provide shorter responses when providing traditional versus accommodated testimony.

Do jurors get what they expect when courts accommodate children in actual cases? In one study, researchers, legal professionals, law enforcement personnel, families of the victims, and victims rated children who testified in court or via CCTV (Cashmore, 1992). Children's behavior changed very little as a function of CCTV use. CCTV children appeared less anxious during their direct examination compared to children who testified in court. During cross-examination, CCTV children appeared more fluent than children in one of the two samples in which CCTV was not used. Yet no differences between children testifying in court versus CCTV emerged for children's confidence, cooperativeness, ability to answer questions, amount of detail provided, or concentration during the direct or cross-examination of the child. Trained observers in a similar study noted few differences in the behavior of traditional versus accommodated testifiers other than that CCTV children were less tearful during cross-examination than children who testified in court (Murray, 1995). Again, observers did not note any differences in children's composure, confidence, concentration, cooperation, or fluency for children providing traditional versus alternative forms of testimony.

Participants in our study expected a child providing alternative testimony to be more confident and cooperative, to provide longer responses, and to be less fidgety than a child providing traditional testimony, but research indicates these changes simply do not occur. Thus, accommodated children's behavior may violate jurors' expectancies. It would also appear jurors' expectancies regarding accommodated children being less nervous, less tearful, and more fluent than traditional testifiers may or may not be violated in actual cases given the mixed results of previous studies (Cashmore, 1993; Murray, 1995). Differences for children's nervousness only emerged for cross-examination in one study (Cashmore, 1993). Differences for children's fluency only emerged in one of the two non-CCTV samples included in Cashmore's study and no such differences were noted in Murray's sample. Finally, Murray observed differences involving children's tearfulness but only during cross-examination.

Prospective jurors may hold expectancies that are violated on a more intuitive level as well when courts accommodate children. For example, participants in our study did not expect accommodated children to appear any more rehearsed or less spontaneous than children testifying in a traditional manner. When courts use accommodations, attorneys or other court personnel help familiarize the child with the alternative procedure. This process varies widely from one jurisdiction to the next, ranging from a simple explanation of the alternative procedure to a more detailed demonstration in which children practice using the alternative procedure. Efforts to familiarize children with accommodations may lead children to appear more rehearsed and less spontaneous than those who do not use accommodations, especially when children receive more extensive forms of preparation. By practicing these techniques and simulating the question/answer format of courtroom testimony, children may become more rehearsed and violate jurors' expectancies.

Up to this point we have focused exclusively on differences in prospective jurors' expectancies for children's behavior as a function of traditional versus accommodated testimony. What about the pattern of effects across the different forms of alternative testimony? These also suggest that jurors may hold unrealistic expectancies regarding the effects of different accommodations on children's testimony. Even though participants in our study expected videotaped children to appear more tearful and less confident than CCTV children, raters observed no such differences in the demeanor of children testifying via CCTV and videotaped testimony (Davies et al., 1995). There is also a general trend in the differences that emerged between accommodations on the nervous, tearful, and confident dependent measures. At one end of the continuum, participants expected the child to be the most nervous, most tearful, and least confident when providing traditional live in-court testimony. At the other end, participants expected the child to be the least nervous, least tearful, and most confident when testifying with a support person or CCTV. Participants' expectancies for the child's prepared and videotaped testimony fell somewhere in between these two extremes.

One potential explanation for this pattern of effects is the degree to which an accommodation is perceived to protect or serve as a buffer between the child and the accused. When CCTV is used, the child is physically removed from the defendant's presence and testifies from a remote location outside the courtroom. When a support person is used, the child testifies in the courtroom in the defendant's presence but is accompanied on the witness stand by the support person while testifying. In contrast, preparation and videotaped testimony (at least as described in our survey) place the child in the defendant's presence without any sort of protection or buffer in ways that are more similar to traditional testimony but with the additional provisions of a courtroom tour, meeting the judge/attorneys, asking questions (via preparation) or testifying in a smaller, more intimate environment than open court (via videotape). If jurors use the degree of unprotected physical confrontation with the accused as a heuristic cue when estimating the effects of different testimony conditions on children's behavior, this outcome would be consistent with research indicating that confronting the defendant is one of the most stressful components of children's testimony (Goodman et al., 1992; Sas, 1991), but at odds with the defendant's constitutional rights and deeply rooted legal jurisprudence concerning the value of confrontation in court (e.g. *Maryland v. Craig,* 1990).

Jurors' beliefs about truth determination, testimony stressfulness, and fairness to trial parties

Participants' beliefs about their enhanced ability to determine children's truthfulness when viewing live versus CCTV or videotaped testimony are largely unsupported by previous research. Studies comparing children's live testimony to videotape testimony (Landström & Granhag, 2010) and live testimony to CCTV testimony (Landström & Granhag, 2010; Orcutt et al., 2001) did not find significant differences in adults' ability to detect children's truthfulness as a function of testimony condition. Participants seemed particularly optimistic about their ability to determine children's truthfulness in the live condition (average rating of 5.75 on a seven-point scale) given that adults generally perform just slightly above chance levels on this task (see Vrij, 2002, for a review).

Prospective jurors' beliefs about the ability of certain accommodations to decrease children's stress are more in line with the empirical literature. Participants believed that all forms of alternative testimony would be less stressful for children than testifying live in court. This finding is consistent with the views of judges (Hafemeister, 1996), prosecuting attorneys (Goodman et al., 1999), and victim witness assistants (McAuliff et al., in press) regarding the ability of support persons, CCTV, and videotape to reduce children's stress while testifying. These views also are consistent with the results of experimental and quasi-experimental research comparing children's traditional versus prepared (Sas, 1991, 1993), videotape (Davies et al., 1995), and CCTV testimony (Cashmore, 1992; Davies & Noon, 1988; Goodman et al., 1998; Landström & Granhag, 2010; Murray, 1995). More difficult to assess, however, are participants' beliefs that certain accommodations are more effective than others at reducing children's stress while testifying. Prosecuting attorneys (Goodman et al., 1999) and judges (Hafemeister, 1996) agree with jurors that support person use decreases children's stress more effectively than CCTV, but no experimental studies have compared these two accommodations. To our knowledge, only one study has randomly assigned children to different alternative testimony conditions (CCTV versus videotape), and no differences in children's self-reported stress emerged between the CCTV and videotaped conditions (Landström & Granhag, 2010).

Participants believed that traditional testimony was the least fair to children compared to all other forms of testimony. In contrast, they believed that traditional testimony was the most fair to defendants compared to prepared and videotaped testimony, but no less fair than support person or CCTV testimony. As a whole, these beliefs generally are not supported by research. Recall that studies asking participants to rate fairness directly did not reveal differences as a function of testimony condition (Lindsay et al., 1995; Swim et al., 1993) and neither did experimental work using more indirect measures (Eaton et al., 2001; Lindsay et al., 1999; Ross et al., 1994; Swim et al., 1993). Some sort of 'buffer heuristic' could be producing the effects seen for participants' expectancies regarding children's nervousness, tearfulness, confidence and their beliefs about children's stress, with those viewing a higher degree of unprotected physical confrontation with the accused as more unfair to the child. Participants' belief that traditional testimony is the fairest to defendants is consistent with legal precedent and the defendant's constitutional right under the Sixth Amendment to confront his accuser.

Limitations

Certain limitations must be acknowledged. We manipulated testimony format within- as opposed to between-participants. A within-participants design increases power and decreases the error variance associated with individual differences, but carry-over and contrast effects may also arise. To minimize this possibility, we counterbalanced the order of the testimony conditions across participants. Separate analyses with order as an independent variable failed to reveal any significant interactions with testimony condition or any of the other independent variables. If carry-over or contrast effects were present in our study, they did not appear to systematically influence participants' expectancies or beliefs.

Our data reflect expectancies and beliefs that participants expressed after reading the brief testimony condition descriptions we provided. We based these descriptions on a review of relevant legislation and case law (McAuliff & Kovera, 2002), but wide variability exists across states and even within jurisdictions with respect to children's testimony and how innovations are defined and implemented. Our descriptions reflect what we considered to be prototypical examples of the different testimony formats and they may vary in some ways from those used in actual cases. For example, our support person condition described the support person sitting next to the child on the stand, but a recent national survey found that this occurs only rarely or sometimes (McAuliff et al., in press). We do not know whether participants' expectancies and beliefs in our study generalize beyond the testimony conditions they read. Also, because our survey described a female victim, our data cannot speak to whether or how prospective jurors' expectancies for testimony behavior might vary based on the child's gender or other witness characteristics.

To some degree, the conclusions we have drawn about what jurors expect versus actually observe when children testify are only as valid as the research to which we compare our data (Cashmore, 1993; Murray, 1995). These studies of the effects of accommodation on child witness behavior are quasi-experimental. As a result, children were not randomly assigned to traditional versus innovative testimony conditions and researchers cannot entirely rule out the influence of confounding variables. Attorneys may be more likely to use accommodations in cases involving severe abuse or when children are extremely reluctant to testify. If so, then it is difficult for researchers to disentangle how these factors influence children's behavior apart from the format of their testimony. Another complicating factor was that our survey included a large number of highly specific behavioral items (smile/frown, timid/brave, fearful/fearless, still/restless), whereas studies examining children's actual testimony included a fewer number of behavioral items and these tended to be more general (observer ratings of children's stress, confidence, happiness). Our conclusions will require updating as the dependent measures used in real-world and laboratory research on children's innovative testimony continue to evolve.

Future directions and conclusion

Like others in the field (e.g. Schmidt & Brigham, 1996), we believe that expectancies for children's behavior can play an important role in understanding jurors' evaluations of children and their testimony. Accommodations are widely available and can lead to beneficial effects in abuse cases by reducing children's stress and increasing their accuracy. However, researchers must continue to explore how accommodations may alter children's verbal and nonverbal behavior in ways that violate jurors' expectancies because such violations may cause jurors to evaluate children negatively and diminish the impact of trial testimony. At a broader level, our data suggest that children who do not appear nervous, tearful, or fidgety or who appear confident, maintain eye contact, and speak fluently may be at risk for violating jurors' expectancies no matter what form of testimony they provide. Using a simulation paradigm to systematically vary the presence or absence of these expected behaviors will allow researchers to adopt a preferable *a priori* approach – *predicting* differences based on known expectancies – versus a less desirable *post hoc* approach – *explaining* differences based on suspected expectancies. Simulation studies will also help improve our knowledge of how jurors react to expectancy violations involving behaviors other than children's crying, which has been documented in previous research (Golding, Fryman, Marsil, & Yozwiak, 2003; Regan & Baker, 1998).

Last but not least, incorporating more objective measures of specific behaviors related to stress, fear, and intimidation will help improve our knowledge of how these states manifest themselves in children providing traditional versus accommodated testimony. Some child witness researchers have moved in this direction by collecting physiological data (Saywitz, Nathanson, Snyder, & Lamphear, 1993; Yim, Quas, Cahill, & Hayakawa, 2010), but measures of more overt behaviors such as a child's eye contact, tearfulness, fidgeting, response latency, and response length also are needed if we truly wish to understand the effects of expectancy violation on jurors' evaluations of child witnesses in laboratory and real-world settings.

Acknowledgements

The first author was supported by Award Number R15HD065651 from the Eunice Kennedy Shriver Institute of Child Health and Human Development during the writing of this manuscript. The content is solely the responsibility of the authors and does not necessarily represent the official views of the Eunice Kennedy Shriver Institute of Child Health and Human Development or the National Institutes of Health. We would like to thank the jury administration staff and personnel at Broward County Courthouse, Seventeenth Judicial District, Fort Lauderdale, Florida (Honorable Robert L. Andrews, Dolly Gibson, Norman Houghtaling, Pat Todaro, Lisa Muggeo, Audrey Edwards, Marvin Edelstein, and Allison Mitchel) for granting us access to the jury pool.

Notes

1. This main effect was qualified by a statistically significant Child Age × Allegation Veracity × Testimony Condition interaction, $F(8, 988) = 2.02$, $p = 0.04$, $\eta_p^2 = 0.02$. When the child's allegation was false, the Child Age × Testimony Condition interaction was not statistically significant. When the child's allegation was true, this two-way interaction was statistically significant. Among participants in the true allegation condition, the pattern of nervousness effects in the 5- and 10-year-old child conditions mirrored that of the main effect means. In the 15-year-old child condition, however, only the difference between the traditional live in-court testimony and support person conditions was significant: participants expected the 15-year-old child to be more nervous when testifying in a traditional manner than when accompanied by a support person.

2. This main effect was qualified by a statistically significant Child Age × Abuse Type × Testimony Condition interaction, $F(8, 976) = 2.30$, $p = 0.02$, $\eta_p^2 = 0.02$. When the alleged abuse was penetration, the Child Age × Testimony Condition interaction was not statistically significant. When the alleged abuse was fondling, this two-way interaction was statistically significant. For participants in the fondling condition, the pattern of stressfulness effects in the 10- and 15-year-old child conditions was identical to that of the main effect means. In the 5-year-old condition, however, the pattern of effects changed such that the difference between CCTV testimony and every other testimony condition was statistically significant.

3. This main effect was qualified by a statistically significant Child Age × Testimony Condition interaction, $F(8, 972) = 2.59$, $p = 0.01$, $\eta_p^2 = 0.02$. The pattern of effects for participants' fairness ratings in the 5- and 10-year-old child conditions mirrored that of the main effect means; however, in the 15-year-old child condition, the differences between the perceived fairness of prepared versus live and videotaped testimony were no longer statistically significant.

References

Ask, K., & Landström, S. (2010). Why emotions matter: Expectancy violation and affective response mediate the emotional victim effect. *Law and Human Behavior, 34*, 392–401. doi:10.1007/s10979-009-9208-6

Burgoon, J.K. (1993). Interpersonal expectations, expectancy violations, and emotional communication. *Journal of Language and Social Psychology, 12*, 30–48. doi:10.1177/0261927X93121003

Burgoon, J.K., & Hale, J.L. (1988). Nonverbal expectancy violations: Model elaboration and application to immediacy behaviors. *Communication Monographs, 55*, 58–79. doi:10.1080/03637758809376158

Burgoon, J.K., & LePoire, B.A. (1993). Effects of communication expectancies, actual communication, and expectancy disconfirmation on evaluations of communicators and their communication behavior. *Human Communication Research, 20*, 67–96. doi:10.1111/j.1468–2958.1993.tb00316.x

Burgoon, J.K., & Walther, J.B. (1990). Nonverbal expectancies and the evaluative consequences of violations. *Human Communication Research, 17*, 232–265. doi:10.1111/j.1468-2958.1990.tb00232.x

Cashmore, J. (1992). *The use of closed-circuit television for child witnesses in the ACT.* Sydney, New South Wales: Australian Law Reform Commission.

Davies, G. (1999). The impact of television on the presentation and reception of children's testimony. *Journal of Law and Psychiatry, 22*, 241–256. doi:10.1016/S0160-2527(99)00007-2

Davies, G., & Noon, E. (1991). *An evaluation of the live link for child witnesses.* London: Home Office.

Davies, G., Wilson, C., Mitchell, R., & Milsom, J. (1995). *Videotaping children's evidence: An evaluation.* London: Home Office.

Eaton, T.E., Ball, P.J., & O'Callaghan, M.G. (2001). Child-witness and defendant credibility: Child evidence presentation mode and judicial instructions. *Journal of Applied Social Psychology, 31*, 1845–1858. doi:10.1111/j.1559–1816.2001.tb00207.x

Feldman, R.S., & Chesley, R.B. (1984). Who is lying, who is not: An attributional analysis of the effects of nonverbal behavior on judgments of defendant believability. *Behavioral Sciences and the Law, 2*, 451–461. doi:10.1002/bsl.2370020411

Golding, J.M., Fryman, H.M., Marsil, D.F., & Yozwiak, J.A. (2003). Big girls don't cry: The effect of witness demeanor on juror decisions in a child sexual abuse trial. *Child Abuse and Neglect, 27*, 1311–1321. doi:10.1016/j.chiabu.2003.03.001

Goodman, G.S., Quas, J.A., Bulkley, J., & Shapiro, C. (1999). Innovations for child witnesses: A national survey. *Psychology, Public Policy, and Law, 5*, 255–281. doi:10.1037/1076-8971.5.2.255

Goodman, G.S., Taub, E.P., Jones, D.P.H., England, P., Port, L.K., Rudy, L., & Prado, L. (1992). Testifying in criminal court. *Monographs of the Society for Research in Child Development, 57* (5, Serial No. 229), 1–142. doi:10.2307/1166127

Goodman, G.S., Tobey, A.E., Batterman-Faunce, J.M., Orcutt, H., Thomas, S., Shapiro, C., & Sachsenmaier, T. (1998). Face-to-face confrontation: Effects of closed circuit-technology on children's eyewitness testimony and jurors' decisions. *Law and Human Behavior, 22*, 165–203. doi:10.1023/A:1025742119977

Hafemeister, T.L. (1996). Protecting child witnesses: Judicial efforts to minimize trauma and reduce evidentiary barriers. *Violence and Victims, 11*, 71–92.

Hall, S.R., & Sales, B.D. (2008). Courtroom modifications for child witnesses: Law and science in forensic evaluations. Washington, DC: American Psychological Association. doi:10.1037/11808-000

Heider, F. (1958). *The psychology of interpersonal relations.* New York, NY: Wiley. doi:10.1037/10628-000

Kelley, H.H. (1972). Attribution in social interaction. In E.E. Jones, D.E. Kanouse, H.H. Kelley, R.E. Nisbett, S. Valins, & B. Weiner (Eds.), *Attribution: Perceiving the causes of behavior* (pp. 151–174). Morristown, NJ: General Learning Press.

Kovera, M.B., Gresham, A.W., Borgida, E., Gray, E., & Regan, P.C. (1997). Does expert testimony inform or influence juror decision-making? A social cognitive analysis. *Journal of Applied Psychology, 82*, 178–191. doi:10.1037/0021-9010.82.1.178

Landström, S., & Granhag, P.A. (2008). Children's truthful and deceptive testimonies: How camera perspective affects adult observers' perception and assessment. *Psychology, Crime & Law, 14*, 381–396. doi:10.1080/10683160701580107

Landström, S., & Granhag, P.A. (2010). In-court versus out-of-court testimonies: Children's experiences and adults' assessments. *Applied Cognitive Psychology, 24*, 941–955. doi:10.1002/acp.1606

Landström, S., Granhag, P.A., & Hartwig, M. (2007). Children's live and videotaped testimonies: How presentation mode affects observers' perception, assessment and memory. *Legal and Criminological Psychology, 12*, 333–347. doi:10.1348/135532506X133607

Lindsay, R.C.L., Ross, D.F., Lea, J.A., & Carr, C. (1995). What's fair when a child testifies? *Journal of Applied Social Psychology, 25*, 870–888. doi:10.1111/j.1559-1816.1995.tb02650.x

Maryland v. Craig, 497 U.S. 836 (1990).

McAuliff, B.D., & Kovera, M.B. (2002). The status of evidentiary and procedural innovations in child abuse proceedings. In B.L. Bottoms, M.B. Kovera, & B.D. McAuliff (Eds.), *Children, social science, and the law* (pp. 412–445). New York, NY: Cambridge University Press. doi:10.1017/CBO9780511500114

McAuliff, B.D., Nicholson, E., Amarilio, D., & Ravanshenas, D.(in press). Supporting children in U.S. legal proceedings: Descriptive and attitudinal data from a national survey of victim/witness assistants. *Psychology, Public Policy, and Law.*

Murray, K. (1995). *Live television link: An evaluation of its use by child witnesses in Scottish criminal trials.* Edinburgh: Scottish Office, Central Research Unit.

Nisbett, R.E., & Ross, L. (1980). *Human inference: Strategies and shortcomings of social judgment.* Englewood Cliffs, NJ: Prentice Hall.

Plotnikoff, J., & Woolfson, R. (2000). *An evaluation of child witness support.* Edinburgh: Scottish Executive Central Research Unit.

Quas, J.A., DeCicco, V., Bulkley, J., & Goodman, G.S. (1996). District attorneys' views of legal innovations for child witnesses. *American Psychology–Law Society Newsletter, 16*, 5–8.

Quas, J.A., Goodman, G.S., Ghetti, S., Alexander, K.W., Edelstein, R., Redlich, A.D.... Jones, D.P.H. (2005). Childhood sexual assault victims: Long-term outcomes after testifying in criminal court. *Monographs of the Society for Research in Child Development, 70* (2, Serial No. 280), 1–128. doi:10.1111/j.1540-5834.2005.00337.x

Regan, P.C., & Baker, S.J. (1998). The impact of child witness demeanor on perceived credibility and trial outcome in sexual abuse cases. *Journal of Family Violence, 13,* 187–195. doi:10.1023/A:1022845724226

Ross, D.F., Hopkins, S., Hanson, E., Lindsay, R.C.L., Hazen, K., & Eslinger, T. (1994). The impact of protective shields and videotape testimony on conviction rates in a simulated trial of child sexual abuse. *Law and Human Behavior, 18,* 553–566. doi:10.1007/BF01499174

Salekin, R.T., Ogloff, J.R.P., McFarland, C., & Rogers, R. (1995). Influencing jurors' perceptions of guilt: Expression of emotionality during testimony. *Behavioral Sciences and the Law, 13,* 293–305. doi:10.1002/bsl.2370130208

Sandler, J.C. (2006). Alternative methods of child testimony: A review of law and research. In C.R. Bartol & A.M. Bartol (Eds.), *Current perspectives in forensic psychology and criminal justice* (pp. 203–214). Thousand Oaks, CA: Sage.

Sas, L.D. (1991). *Reducing the system-induced trauma for child sexual abuse victims through court preparation, assessment and follow-up* (Final Report, Project No. 4555-1-125, National Welfare Grants Division, Health and Welfare Canada). London, Ontario: London Family Court Clinic.

Sas, L.D. (1993). *Three years after the verdict: A longitudinal study of the social and psychological adjustment of child witnesses referred to the child witness project* (Final Report, Project No. 4887-06-91-026, Family Violence Prevention Division of Health Canada). London, Ontario: London Family Court Clinic.

Saywitz, K.J., Nathanson, R., Snyder, L., & Lamphear, V. (1993). *Preparing children for the investigative and judicial process: Improving communication, memory, and emotional resiliency* (Final Report to the National Center on Child Abuse and Neglect, Grant No. 90-CA-1179). Los Angeles, CA: University of California.

Saywitz, K.J., & Nathanson, R. (1993). Children's testimony and their perceptions of stress in and out of the courtroom. *Child Abuse and Neglect, 17,* 613–622. doi:10.1016/0145-2134(93)90083-H

Schmidt, C.W., & Brigham, J.C. (1996). Jurors' perceptions of child victim-witnesses in a simulated sexual abuse trial. *Law and Human Behavior, 20,* 581–606. doi:10.1007/BF01499233

Sigler, R.T., Crowley, J.M., & Johnson, I. (1990). Judicial and prosecutorial endorsement of innovative techniques in the trial of domestic abuse cases. *Journal of Criminal Justice, 18,* 443–453. doi:10.1016/0047-2352(90)90059-K

Swim, J.K., Borgida, E., & McCoy, K. (1993). Videotaped versus in-court witness testimony: Does protecting the child witnesses jeopardize due process? *Journal of Applied Social Psychology, 23,* 603–631. doi:10.1111/j.1559-1816.1993.tb01105.x

Tobey, A.E., Goodman, G.S., Batterman-Faunce, J.M., Orcutt, H.K., & Sachsenmaier, T. (1995). Balancing the rights of children and defendants: Effects of closed-circuit television on children's accuracy and jurors' perceptions. In M.S. Zaragoza, J.R. Graham, G.C.N. Hall, R. Hirschman, & Y.S. Ben-Porath (Eds.), *Memory and testimony in the child witness* (pp. 214–239). Thousand Oaks, CA: Sage.

Vrij, A. (2002). Deception in children: A literature review and implications for children's testimony. In H.L. Westcott, G.M. Davies, & R.H.C. Bull (Eds.), *Children's testimony: A handbook of psychological research and forensic practice* (pp. 175–194). Chichester: Wiley. doi:10.1002/9780470713679

Whitcomb, D. (1992). *When the victim is a child* (2nd ed.). Washington, DC: US Department of Justice.

Yim, I.S.,Quas, J.A.,Cahill, L., &Hayakawa, C.M.(2010). Children's and adults' salivary cortisol responses to an identical psychosocial laboratory stressor. *Psychoneuroendocrinology, 35,* 241–248. doi:10.1016/j.psyneuen.2009.06.014

The effects of mock jurors' beliefs about eyewitness performance on trial judgments

Tess M.S. Neal[a], Ashley Christiansen[b], Brian H. Bornstein[b] and
Timothy R. Robicheaux[c]

[a]Department of Psychology, The University of Alabama, Tuscaloosa, AL, USA; [b]Department of
Psychology, University of Nebraska–Lincoln, Lincoln, Nebraska, USA; [c]Department of
Psychology, The Pennsylvania State University, University Park, Pennsylvania, USA

Two experiments examined how mock jurors' beliefs about three factors known to
influence eyewitness memory accuracy relate to decision making (age of
eyewitness and presence of weapon in Study 1, length of eyewitness identification
decision time in Study 2). Psychology undergraduates rendered verdicts and
evaluated trial participants after reading a robbery–murder trial summary that
varied eyewitness age (6, 11, 42, or 74 years) and weapon presence (visible or not)
in Study 1 and eyewitness decision length (2–3 or 30 s) in Study 2 ($n = 200$ each).
The interactions between participant belief about these variables and the
manipulated variables themselves were the heart of this study. Participants'
beliefs about eyewitness age and weapon presence interacted with these
manipulations, but only for some judgments – verdict for eyewitness age and
eyewitness credibility for weapon focus. The exploratory meditational analyses
found only one relation: juror belief about eyewitness age mediated the relation
between eyewitness age and credibility ratings. These results highlight a need for
juror education and specialized *voir dire* in cases where legitimate concerns exist
regarding the reliability of eyewitness memory (e.g. child eyewitness, weapon
presence during event, long eyewitness identification time). If erroneous juror
beliefs can be corrected their impact may be reduced.

Introduction

Eyewitness evidence is one of the most compelling types of evidence presented at
trial, as jurors place great weight on the testimony of eyewitnesses (Devenport,
Penrod, & Cutler, 1997; Lindsay, 1994; Penrod & Cutler, 1995). However, laypeople
are often naive to the value of various predictors of eyewitness memory accuracy, the
consequences of which may be jurors making judgments based in part on erroneous
intuitions (Benton, Ross, Bradshaw, Thomas, & Bradshaw, 2006; Deffenbacher &
Loftus, 1982; Devenport et al., 1997; Kassin & Barndollar, 1992; Lindsay, 1994;
Read & Desmarais, 2009). For instance, jurors assume a positive correlation between
eyewitness confidence and accuracy; in fact, the most powerful predictor of mock
jurors' verdicts is eyewitness confidence (Cutler, Penrod, & Dexter, 1990; Cutler,

49

Penrod, & Stuve, 1988). However, contrary to jurors' beliefs, eyewitness confidence is not a strong indicator of accuracy (Penrod & Cutler, 1995; Sporer, Penrod, Read, & Cutler, 1995).

Other research has demonstrated potential jurors do not appreciate many factors related to eyewitness accuracy. For example, the impact of the cross-race effect or how lineup instructions can affect eyewitness identification is not well understood (Lindsay, 1994); the ability of hypnosis to aid memory retrieval is overestimated, and the effects of exposure time, lineup selection procedures, and hypnotic suggestibility are underestimated (Kassin & Barndollar, 1992); and arousal's negative impact on accurate recall is not appreciated (Bornstein, Zickafoose, & O'Bryant, 2008). Other factors that may predict eyewitness accuracy include age of the eyewitness, whether or not a weapon was present during the occurrence of the crime, and the length of time it takes the eyewitness to identify a perpetrator during a lineup. Researchers have examined the effects of these variables on juror decisions; however, jurors' beliefs about these variables and the effects of those beliefs on decisions have not been empirically examined.

Age of the eyewitness

An abundance of research has addressed age effects on eyewitness memory. The ability to retain accurate descriptive information in memory after witnessing an event increases with age (Leippe & Romanczyk, 1989; Poole & White, 1991; Roebers & Schneider, 2001), as does accurate face identification (Pozzulo & Lindsay, 1998). However, elderly adults perform significantly worse than younger adults at face-recognition tasks (Bartlett & Memon, 2007), and they have less accurate memories and are disproportionately influenced by erroneous suggestions compared to younger adults (Mueller-Johnson, 2005). Thus it appears young to middle adulthood is the peak age range for eyewitness performance accuracy.

Laypeople regard the age of an eyewitness as important for determining the accuracy of eyewitness identification (Golding, Dunlap, & Hodell, 2009; Holcomb & Jacquin, 2007; Leippe, Manion, & Romanczyk, 1992; Newcombe & Bransgrove, 2007; Pozzulo & Dempsey, 2009; Pozzulo, Lemieux, Wells, & McCuaig, 2006; Ross, Dunning, Toglia, & Ceci, 1990). However, surveys assessing experts' (Kassin, Tubb, Hosch, & Memon, 2001) and laypersons' (Benton et al., 2006) beliefs about factors affecting eyewitness accuracy demonstrate experts are significantly more likely to agree that young children and elderly eyewitnesses are less accurate than younger adults, indicating jurors may rely on erroneous beliefs in decision making.

A number of jury simulations have examined the effect of eyewitness age on mock jurors' decisions, especially in the context of child sexual abuse (CSA) cases (Bottoms, Golding, Stevenson, Wiley, & Yozwiak, 2007), where a majority of jurors cite the child's testimony as the most important evidence (Myers, Redlich, Goodman, Prizmich, & Imwinkelried, 1999). Jurors generally perceive younger children as less cognitively capable than older children or adults, but as more trustworthy and honest; in the case of CSA or other sex crimes, children's credibility is also aided by the perception that they are more sincere and sexually naive (Bottoms et al., 2007). Less research has studied jurors' perceptions of elderly witnesses, but there is evidence that they are perceived as less cognitively capable yet more honest than young adults (Ross et al., 1990).

The weapon focus effect

A second factor demonstrated to predict eyewitness accuracy is weapon presence during the commission of a crime. The presence of a weapon can reduce the ability to recall details unrelated to the weapon (e.g. clothing and characteristics of the suspect; Pickel, 2007; Shaw & Skolnick, 1994; Steblay, 1992), and reduces the probability of an eyewitness identifying the offender (Pickel, 2007). Surveys assessing expert (Kassin et al., 2001) and laypersons' (Benton et al., 2006; Read & Desmarais, 2009) beliefs about factors affecting eyewitness accuracy indicate that experts better appreciate memory limitations when a weapon is present, suggesting again that jurors may make decisions based partially on erroneous beliefs. However, we know of no studies of juror or jury decision making as a function of weapon presence/absence.

Length of identification time during lineups

A third factor that predicts the accuracy of eyewitness identification is the length of time the identification takes during a lineup. Faster identifications are, in general, more likely to be correct than slower decisions (Dunning & Stern, 1994; Sauerland & Sporer, 2009; Sporer, 1993, 1994). Nevertheless, there is considerable variability in opinions about identification speed (Benton et al., 2006; Read & Desmarais, 2009). The pattern suggests many mock jurors believe fast identifications are more accurate and may base decisions on that belief; however, there is not a strong expert consensus on whether identification speed has any relation to accuracy, despite several studies suggesting such a relationship. In addition, there have been no studies of how mock jurors respond to variations in eyewitness identification speed.

The present research

We conducted two studies to determine how mock jurors' beliefs about three factors relate to their decision making (age of the eyewitness and presence of a weapon in Study 1, and length of eyewitness identification decision time in Study 2). We chose these three factors not because they exhaust all of the factors about which jurors might have erroneous beliefs, but because of their prevalence in a large number of witnessing and identification situations. In these studies, college students serving as mock jurors read a simulated criminal trial in which we varied the level of the three variables (eyewitness age, weapon presence, and identification time) to determine whether mock jurors' beliefs were related to their trial decisions.

Study 1: eyewitness age and weapon presence

Study 1 examined the relations between mock jurors' judgments and their beliefs regarding eyewitness age and weapon presence. Overall, we hypothesized mock jurors would be somewhat sensitive to these factors, and that their beliefs would be related to their trial judgments. Specifically, we predicted: (1) A main effect of eyewitness age, such that more not-guilty verdicts will be rendered when the eyewitness is a child or elderly adult (compared with a middle-aged adult). Young and elderly adult eyewitnesses will also be less credible, and will lead to perceptions of lower defendant culpability. Although child and elderly witnesses can be quite credible when the major component of credibility is their honesty or sincerity (e.g. in CSA cases), they are less credible than young adult witnesses when the case emphasizes cognitive competence (Bottoms et al., 2007). In the case used here, the eyewitness is a bystander with no motivation to lie, leading to the predicted age effect. (2) A main effect of weapon presence, such that weapon presence will lead to more not guilty verdicts, lower defendant culpability, and lower eyewitness credibility. (3) An interaction between eyewitness age and participant belief about the effects of eyewitness age on reliability. Specifically, participants who believe younger eyewitnesses are less reliable will render more negative judgments when a younger eyewitness testifies compared to the middle-age condition, whereas participants who believe younger eyewitnesses are more reliable will render more positive judgments when a younger eyewitness testifies compared to the middle-age condition. (4) An interaction between weapon presence and participant belief in the weapon focus effect. Specifically, participants who believe weapon presence interferes with memories of the event unrelated to the weapon (i.e. those who believe in the weapon focus effect) will render more negative judgments when a weapon is present compared to when it is not. Participants who do not believe in the weapon focus effect will render more positive judgments when a weapon is present compared to when it is not.

Method

Participants

Two hundred jury-eligible undergraduate students (60.5% female) at the University of Nebraska–Lincoln participated. Participants were representative of the university's population (mean age = 19.84, 88% White). Recruitment took place through the psychology department's internet-based subject pool. Participants received course credit for participation.

Materials and procedure

Each participant, through random assignment, received one of eight versions of a criminal trial summary. A 2 × 4 between-groups factorial design was utilized to examine effects of eyewitness age (6, 11, 42, or 74 years) and weapon presence (weapon visible or not) on mock jurors' decisions. The trial summary described a convenience store robbery in which an eyewitness observed a culprit either with or without a gun. The eyewitness was the only person with a clear view of the robbery, and he claimed to remember what the perpetrator looked like and was able to pick the alleged robber out of a lineup. The eyewitness testified that the defendant was the person who robbed the store.

Participants were first asked to fill out a questionnaire concerning beliefs and attitudes about the legal system, which included questions about participants' beliefs about the effects of eyewitness age and weapon presence on eyewitness reliability (Deffenbacher & Loftus, 1982). These questions were rated on a 1 (*strongly disagree*) to 5 (*strongly agree*) point scale. Participants with higher values on the child eyewitness reliability item (e.g. 'A child eyewitness is more reliable than an adult eyewitness') endorsed a stronger belief in the reliability of child eyewitnesses compared to those with lower values (i.e. low values were more consistent with the empirical literature). Participants with higher values on the weapon focus effect question endorsed a stronger belief in the effect ('When a person sees a weapon while witnessing a crime, s/he will have a reduced ability to remember the details of the event'; i.e. high values were more consistent with the empirical literature).

After reading the transcript, participants completed additional questionnaires. They provided demographic information, a verdict, and rated the credibility of the witnesses (1, *low* to 5, *high*).[1] In addition to the dichotomous verdict decision, participants also rated the perceived culpability of the defendant (0–100%).

Results

Please refer to Table 1 for descriptive statistics. We examined whether participant age, gender, or race moderated any of our effects. They did not, so we did not include them in our models. To examine our hypotheses about verdict decision, we performed a binary logistic regression. Predictors included eyewitness age (categorical), weapon presence (categorical), participant belief about the effect of eyewitness age and weapon presence on accuracy (each continuous), and the interactions between eyewitness age × belief about age and weapon presence × belief about weapon presence.

Verdict decision was significantly related to eyewitness age (odds ratio = 0.02, 95% CI = 0.00–0.72, $p = 0.03$). Specifically, the 42-year-old eyewitness elicited fewer not guilty (15%) verdicts compared to child (22% and 23%) and elderly (29%) eyewitnesses. The interaction between eyewitness age and participant belief about the effect of eyewitness age emerged in the predicted direction (odds ratio = 2.66, 95% CI = 0.99–7.13, $p = 0.05$). When the eyewitness was 6 years old, mock jurors who convicted the defendant believed child eyewitnesses were more reliable ($M = 3.32$, SD = 0.84) than those who found the defendant not guilty ($M = 4.10$, SD = 0.87), $t(51) = 3.17$, $p = 0.003$. For eyewitnesses of all other ages, the beliefs of mock jurors who convicted and acquitted did not differ significantly, $ts < 0.9$.

To examine the remaining hypotheses, we conducted a between-groups multivariate analysis of covariance (MANCOVA). We included two categorical independent variables (age of eyewitness and weapon presence), two continuous independent variables entered as covariates (strength of participant belief in child eyewitnesses reliability and the weapon focus effect), and the interactions between eyewitness age × age belief and weapon presence × weapon focus effect belief. The dependent variables were eyewitness credibility and defendant culpability.

The results of the overall omnibus tests were significant for four of the independent variables. We found significant omnibus main effects for eyewitness age, Wilks' Lambda = 0.79, $F(6,382) = 7.83$, $p < 0.001$, $eta_p^2 = 0.11$; strength of participant belief in child eyewitness reliability, Wilks' Lambda = 0.96, $F(2,191) = 3.75$, $p = 0.025$, $eta_p^2 = 0.04$; strength of participant belief in the weapon focus effect, Wilks' Lambda = 0.97, $F(2,191) = 3.32$, $p = 0.038$, $eta_p^2 = 0.03$; and the interaction between weapon presence and the strength of participants' beliefs about the weapon focus effect, Wilks' Lambda = 0.96, $F(2,191) = 3.58$, $p = 0.03$, $eta_p^2 = 0.04$. Nonsignificant effects included the predicted main effect of weapon presence and the predicted interaction between eyewitness age and strength of participant belief in child eyewitness accuracy, Wilks' Lambdas < 0.96, $Fs < 4.32$, $ps > 0.05$, $eta_p^2 < 0.04$.

Table 1. Study 1 Descriptive statistics.

	Measure			
	Defendant culpability (%)		Eyewitness credibility	
	M	SD	M	SD
Prior witness age belief				
Adults more reliable				
6-year-old eyewitness	50.83	28.58	2.57*	0.92
11-year-old eyewitness	59.70	23.90	3.32	0.80
42-year-old eyewitness	68.44	23.47	3.89	0.95
74-year-old eyewitness	53.10	26.20	2.97	1.02
Children more reliable				
6-year-old eyewitness	81.00	31.31	3.80	1.30
11-year-old eyewitness	71.22	28.94	3.56	0.73
42-year-old eyewitness	71.25	16.52	3.75	0.50
74-year-old eyewitness	48.38	25.29	2.63	0.52
Prior witness focus effect belief				
Believes in weapon effect				
Weapon Present	58.50	26.93	3.11†	1.08
Weapon Absent	56.73	29.42	3.41	1.08
Does not believe in weapon effect				
Weapon present	66.10	21.48	3.50	0.98
Weapon absent	65.79	24.89	3.21	1.02

Prior witness age belief: the belief dichotomies represented here were created by recoding the belief variable. Participants indicating agreement (answering 4 or 5) were categorized as 'child believers' ($n = 26$), participants who answered 1 or 2 were categorized as 'non-believers' ($n = 125$), neutral participants are not included ($n = 49$). *Credibility variables were measured on a scale of 1 to 5, with 1 as least credible and 5 as most credible. $N = 151$.

Prior witness focus effect belief: the belief dichotomies represented here were created by recoding the belief variable. Participants indicating agreement (answering 4 or 5) were categorized as 'believers' ($n = 95$), participants who answered 1 or 2 were categorized as 'non-believers' ($n = 57$), and neutral participants are not included here ($n = 48$). †Credibility variables were measured on a scale of 1 to 5, with 1 as least credible and 5 as most credible. $N = 152$.

We further explored these findings by using separate univariate ANCOVAs with follow-up LSD *post hoc* analyses when appropriate. We observed significant univariate effects of age of eyewitness on defendant culpability ratings, $F(3,192) = 5.14$, $p = 0.002$, $eta^2_p = 0.07$. Consistent with our hypothesis, the 42-year-old eyewitness ($M = 70.98$, SD $= 22.69$) elicited significantly higher defendant culpability ratings than the 6-year-old ($M = 56.83$, SD $= 28.99$) and 74-year-old eyewitness ($M = 54.24$, SD $= 25.31$), $p = 0.003$ and <0.001, respectively. We also found significant differences between the eyewitness age groups on credibility ratings, $F(3,192) = 14.00$, $p < 0.001$, $eta^2_p = 0.18$. The 42-year-old eyewitness elicited significantly higher ratings ($M = 3.94$, SD $= 0.94$) than any of the other three groups, $p < 0.002$.

Although we did not formulate any *a priori* hypotheses regarding main effects of participant beliefs, we found significant univariate effects for the strength of belief that child eyewitnesses are more accurate than adults on both defendant culpability ratings (β = 5.22, t = 2.73, p = 0.007, eta_p^2 = 0.04) and eyewitness credibility ratings (β = 0.15, t = 2.12, p = 0.036, eta_p^2 = 0.02). The positive relation between defendant culpability ratings and child eyewitness accuracy belief indicates that for each unit increase participants endorsed on the five-point child eyewitness accuracy belief item, culpability ratings for the defendant increased by 5.22%. The relation between child eyewitness accuracy belief and eyewitness credibility ratings indicates that for each unit increase participants endorsed on the five-point child eyewitness accuracy item, eyewitness credibility ratings increased by 0.15 units on the 1–5 scale. No significant main effect was found for strength of weapon focus belief on either defendant culpability ratings or eyewitness credibility ratings (βs < 4.18, ts < 1.87, ps > 0.06).

We hypothesized an interaction between participants' beliefs and the manipulated conditions (age and weapon presence) consistent with their beliefs. As explained above, no relations between eyewitness age and strength of participant belief in child eyewitness reliability were found. Likewise, the predicted interaction between weapon presence and strength of participant belief in the weapon focus effect did not emerge for defendant culpability ratings, β = 0.88, t = 0.27, p = 0.79, eta_p^2 < 0.001. However, the predicted interaction between weapon presence and strength of participant belief in the weapon focus effect did emerge for eyewitness credibility, β = 0.26, t = 2.10, p = 0.037, eta_p^2 = 0.02. A stronger belief in the weapon focus effect was associated with higher eyewitness credibility ratings when the weapon was absent, but with lower credibility ratings when the weapon was present (see Figure 1).

We conducted exploratory analyses to see whether juror beliefs mediated the relation between the independent variables (eyewitness age, weapon presence) and the continuous dependent variables (eyewitness credibility, defendant culpability). Baron and Kenny's (1986) method and Sobel (1982) tests were used to explore these relationships, which produced identical findings (we present only the Baron and Kenny analysis here). Although we explored four potential meditational models, only one emerged as significant. We found support for juror beliefs about the effect of eyewitness age as a mediator between eyewitness age and credibility.

As per Baron and Kenny's (1986) method, regression analyses found that eyewitness age (the independent variable) accounted for a significant portion of variance in juror belief (the mediator), β = 0.22, $t(199)$ = 3.18, p = 0.002, and eyewitness age (independent variable) significantly predicted eyewitness credibility (dependent variable), β = 0.17, $t(199)$ = 2.41, p = 0.017. In a separate model testing the relations between both the independent variable and the mediator on the dependent variable, the mediator (juror belief) remained significant, β = 0.27, $t(199)$ = 3.89, p < 0.001, whereas the effect of the independent variable (eyewitness age) was no longer significant, β = 0.11, $t(44)$ = 1.57, p = 0.12, indicating that full mediation was demonstrated.

Discussion

This study examined the relation between mock jurors' judgments and beliefs regarding eyewitness age and weapon presence. Consistent with our hypotheses, mock jurors were generally sensitive to these factors, and beliefs were related to trial

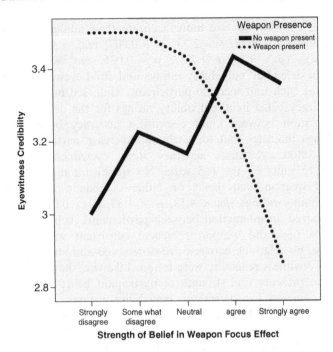

Figure 1. Weapon presence and weapon focus belief interaction on eyewitness credibility.

judgments. A main effect of eyewitness age emerged on verdict, defendant culpability, and eyewitness credibility ratings, such that the adult eyewitness elicited significantly fewer not guilty verdicts and elicited higher culpability and credibility ratings compared to child and elderly eyewitnesses. These findings are encouraging, as they are consistent with empirical findings that adults are better eyewitnesses than both children (Pozzulo & Lindsay, 1998; Poole & White, 1991; Roebers & Schneider, 2001) and elderly adults (Bartlett & Memon, 2007; Mueller-Johnson, 2005).

Although verdict decisions showed the predicted interaction between eyewitness age and participant belief, ratings of culpability and credibility did not. This may indicate jurors were indeed affected by the independent variables (as evidenced by the differential verdict decisions), but that the effect did not significantly influence lower order judgments – the culpability and credibility ratings. Other research has found a similar pattern of results: although successful manipulations may affect verdict or credibility ratings, one does not always translate into the other as a function of the manipulation (e.g. Abshire & Bornstein, 2003; Lindsay, 1994).

Unexpectedly, a significant main effect was found for strength of participant belief in child eyewitness reliability on both defendant culpability and eyewitness credibility ratings. Both increased as participant endorsement of child eyewitness reliability increased. This finding suggests mock jurors naive to the limitations of child eyewitness reliability are also likely to believe witnesses are more credible and defendants are more culpable in general. Less knowledgeable jurors may hold erroneous beliefs that influence broad trial perceptions. Surveys assessing beliefs about eyewitness age and reliability suggest jurors are less knowledgeable than experts (Kassin et al., 2001; Benton et al., 2006). It appears in this study that the effects of erroneous juror beliefs about eyewitness age and reliability predict trial perceptions.

We hypothesized a main effect of weapon presence; however, it did not emerge in any of the analyses. This is surprising because the presence of a weapon is known to affect memory for details of the event unrelated to the weapon (Pickel, 2007; Shaw & Skolnick, 1994; Steblay, 1992). The findings are consistent with surveys indicating mock jurors are significantly less knowledgeable about the weapon focus effect than experts (Benton et al., 2006; Kassin et al., 2001; Read & Desmarais, 2009). One possible reason no main effect emerged for weapon presence is because the manipulation may not have been effective. A limitation of this study is that we did not include a manipulation check for either the eyewitness age or weapon presence variable; therefore, it is possible participants did not discern a difference between conditions.

The predicted interactions involving weapon focus were partially supported. Findings suggest mock jurors who hold correct beliefs perceive the credibility of witnesses consistent with the literature (e.g. Pickel, 2007). However, the non-significant interaction for defendant culpability ratings or verdict indicates the effect of correct beliefs may be limited only to judgments of the eyewitness's credibility. This may be because the weapon focus effect would have the most immediate impact on the eyewitness's memory for the details of the event unrelated to the weapon, whereas judgments of defendant culpability and verdict are more distally related.

Study 2: length of eyewitness identification time

We conducted Study 2 to examine whether, and in what ways, mock juror beliefs about lineup identification speed affect their decisions. Based on the literature, we hypothesized mock jurors would be somewhat sensitive to this factor, and that their beliefs would be related to their trial judgments. Specifically, we predicted: (1) A main effect of length of identification time, such that slower identifications will result in more not guilty verdicts than faster identifications. Slower identifications will also result in lower eyewitness credibility and defendant culpability ratings. (2) An interaction between length of identification time and participant belief about decision time. Specifically, participants who believe faster identifications are more likely to be accurate will render more positive judgments in the fast condition compared to the slow condition and vice versa.

Method

Participants

Two hundred jury-eligible undergraduate students (67% female) at the University of Nebraska–Lincoln participated. Participants were representative of the university's population (mean age = 20.45 years, largely White). Recruitment took place through the psychology department's internet-based subject pool, and participants received course credit.

Design

Participants were randomly assigned to either a relatively long or short eyewitness identification time condition. The strength of participants' beliefs in the accuracy of identification time was measured by their response to an item in a pre-trial questionnaire ('The more quickly an eyewitness identifies a person as the perpetrator in a lineup, the more accurate the identification is likely to be [compared to an identification that takes a longer time]'; Kassin et al., 2001). Participants rated their response on a Likert-type scale, from 1, '*strongly agree*' to 5, '*strongly disagree.*' The dependent variables were the verdict rendered (guilty/not guilty), defendant culpability ratings, (0–100%), and witness credibility ratings (1, *low* to 5, *high*).

Materials

Participants were given a 17-page transcript of a robbery–murder case, with similar case facts to the trial used in Study 1, except for a few minor differences (e.g. the eyewitness in Study 2 was female). The eyewitness' testimony consisted of her report of observing a robbery-murder in a convenience store in which she worked. She was looking out of a window from an office about 20 feet away from the perpetrator. When asked how long it took her to identify the defendant (from a simultaneous lineup), she responded, 'I made my decision as soon as I saw him' in the fast condition, whereas in the slow condition she said, 'I had to think about it for a while before I could be sure of my choice.'

The police officer witness gave a general description of the lineup procedure. Upon cross-examination, he testified about the length of time it took the eyewitness to identify the defendant. In the fast condition he said, 'It was quite fast, 2 or 3 s, maybe.' In the slow condition he said, '[she] debated for about 30 s.' These measures were based on Sporer's (1993) findings that the average 'correct' decision time was 3.47 s and the average 'incorrect' decision time was 13.33 s.

Procedure

Participants read a consent form and were instructed to pretend they had been selected as a juror in the case. They filled out a 20-item Juror Attitude Survey, which included the belief about identification speed item. They were then asked to read the transcript and give their verdict, rate the defendant's culpability and each witness' credibility,[1] and answer a manipulation check question concerning identification speed. The procedure took 30–40 min and was completed individually.

Results

Please refer to Table 2 for descriptive statistics. The manipulation check revealed the eyewitness identification speed manipulation was perceived as intended. Ninety-seven per cent correctly reported their perception of the fast condition as relatively fast, and 61% in the slow condition reported their perception as relatively slow, $X^2(1, 199) = 78.96$, $p < 0.001$, $\kappa = 0.04$. Participants who failed the manipulation check were excluded from further analyses.

Table 2. Study 2 descriptive statistics.

	Measure			
	Defendant culpability (%)		Eyewitness credibility*	
Prior identification speed belief	M	SD	M	SD
Believe speed helps accuracy				
Fast eyewitness decision	60.66	30.77	3.41	1.02
Slow eyewitness decision	52.56	30.87	3.44	1.09
Believes speed hinders accuracy				
Fast eyewitness decision	76.22	26.12	3.83	0.81
Slow eyewitness decision	54.38	25.34	3.08	0.97

Note: the belief dichotomies represented here were created by recoding the belief variable. Participants indicating agreement (answering 1 or 2) were categorized as 'speed believers' ($n = 91$), participants who answered 4 or 5 were categorized as 'slow believers' ($n = 76$), neutral participants are not included ($n = 33$). *Credibility variables were measured on a scale of 1 to 5, with 1 as least credible and 5 as most credible. $N = 131$.

To examine our hypotheses about verdict decision, a binary logistic regression with verdict as the dependent variable and eyewitness identification speed (categorical), strength of participant belief about the effect of identification speed (continuous), and the interaction between the two variables as predictors was computed. Consistent with our hypothesis, the defendant was less likely to be found guilty when the identification was slow (6%) compared to when it was fast (47%) (odds ratio = 55.80, 95% CI = 3.32–937.17, $p = 0.005$). The predicted interaction between length of identification time and participant belief about the effect of length of identification time did not emerge (odds ratio = 0.55, 95% CI = 0.24–1.24, $p = 0.15$).

To examine the remaining hypotheses, we conducted a between-groups multivariate analysis of covariance (MANCOVA). We included one categorical independent variable (identification time), one continuous independent variable entered as a covariate (strength of juror belief that faster identifications are more accurate), and the interaction. Our two continuous dependent variables were defendant culpability and eyewitness credibility. A significant omnibus main effect was found for identification speed, Wilks' Lambda = 0.96, $F(2,152) = 3.61$, $p = 0.029$, $eta_p^2 = 0.05$. The predicted interaction between identification speed and speed belief did not emerge, and no main effect was found for speed belief, Wilks' Lambdas < 1.0, Fs (2, 152) < 1.75, ps > 0.17.

Significant univariate effects of identification speed emerged on defendant culpability ($F(1,153) = 5.68$, $p = 0.018$, $eta_p^2 = 0.04$) and eyewitness credibility ($F(1,153) = 5.45$, $p = 0.021$, $eta_p^2 = 0.03$) ratings. Consistent with our hypotheses, slower identifications were associated with lower culpability ratings ($M = 51.65$, SD = 27.15) than faster identifications ($M = 68.88$, SD = 28.51), and slower identifications elicited lower credibility ratings ($M = 3.32$, SD = 0.98) than faster identifications ($M = 3.62$, SD = 0.93).

As in Study 1, we conducted exploratory analyses to discern whether juror beliefs might mediate the relation between the independent variable (identification decision speed) and the continuous dependent variables (eyewitness credibility, defendant culpability). Baron and Kenny's (1986) method and Sobel (1982) tests were used to explore these potential meditational relationships. Although we explored both potential meditational models, neither emerged as significant; therefore, it does not appear juror beliefs mediate this relation.

Discussion

This study examined the effect of eyewitness identification time on mock juror decisions, including the degree to which intuition about identification time plays a role. Our hypothesis that identification time would emerge as a main effect for each of the dependent variables was supported. This is an encouraging finding, as it is consistent with research findings that faster identifications are more likely to be accurate (e.g. Sauerland & Sporer, 2009).

The null findings for the main effect of participant belief and the interaction between identification time and participant belief may be due to a weak relation between the variables, or it may be because participants underestimate the effects of identification time, as Kassin and Barndollar (1992) found with other eyewitness factors. Alternatively, this can be interpreted as encouraging, because although some jurors indicated a belief that slower identifications are more likely to be accurate, the effect of these erroneous beliefs on judgments was minimal.

The results of the manipulation check showed the identification speed manipulation was perceived as intended. Although this was a 'successful' manipulation statistically, participants in the slow condition made more errors in the manipulation check (39%) than those in the fast condition (3%). Thus, the slow condition manipulation may not have been strong enough to elicit some expected results. Future studies should attempt a more recognizably slow condition to examine the effect on jurors' decisions (e.g. the slow condition could take 3 min rather than 30 s).

General discussion

How well do jurors' beliefs predict trial judgments? Previous research indicates the beliefs with which jurors arrive in court can influence their trial perceptions and decisions (e.g. Bornstein et al., 2008). This reality is problematic for the legal system when juror beliefs are erroneous. We conducted the current studies to examine the effects of juror beliefs regarding problematic situations identified in previous research (e.g. child and elderly eyewitness, weapon focus, and a slow identification).

The main effects of eyewitness age and identification time parallels empirical knowledge regarding how eyewitness age and identification time actually predict eyewitness reliability. Unexpectedly, no main effects of weapon presence emerged, which is not in line with empirical findings that the presence of a weapon negatively affects eyewitness memory for details of the crime and perpetrator identification (Pickel, 2007; Shaw & Skolnick, 1994; Steblay, 1992). However, an interaction between weapon effect belief and weapon presence emerged.

The interactions between the manipulated variables and participant belief about them were the heart of this study. We hypothesized an interaction between the independent variable and the relevant participant belief for each dependent variable. The hypothesis was partially supported, but only for eyewitness age and weapon presence, and only for some judgments – verdict for eyewitness age, and eyewitness credibility for weapon focus. Although it is not clear why these conceptually related dependent variables would have different outcomes, a similar pattern has been obtained by other researchers (e.g. Abshire & Bornstein, 2003; Lindsay, 1994). No interactions were found for identification speed and participant belief. The directions of the significant interactions are in line with what would be expected based on participant belief. These results are both encouraging and discouraging. Juror beliefs do predict at least some perceptions and judgments at trial. This is encouraging when juror beliefs are in line with empirical findings, but discouraging when juror beliefs are erroneous.

The exploratory mediational analyses in each study found only one relation: juror beliefs about eyewitness age significantly mediated the relation between eyewitness age and credibility. It makes theoretical sense that the relation between eyewitness age and credibility would be mediated through juror beliefs about the effects of eyewitness age, because these variables are all directly related. Although it was somewhat surprising that the same pattern was not found when defendant culpability served as the dependent variable, this may be due to the fact that eyewitness credibility is more directly related to the independent variable and dependent variable in this case than is defendant culpability. Likewise, the relations between weapon presence, beliefs about weapon presence, and eyewitness credibility and defendant culpability were not significant mediational relations; nor were relations between identification speed, belief about identification speed, and eyewitness credibility and defendant culpability ratings. This may be because these dependent variables are not as directly relevant to the independent variable and mediator as the eyewitness credibility ratings were for eyewitness age and beliefs about eyewitness age.

The results of this investigation highlight a potential need for juror education concerning factors that can influence eyewitness reliability and accuracy. In cases where legitimate concerns exist regarding the reliability of eyewitness memory (e.g. the eyewitness is a child, a weapon was present during the event, the eyewitness took a long time to identify, etc.), attorneys may be wise to include *voir dire* questions to expose juror beliefs when such beliefs might bear on the case outcome. Although *voir dire* in general is not a particularly effective safeguard (Van Wallendael, Cutler, Devenport, & Penrod, 2007), jurors with problematic expectations about relevant eyewitness issues could be removed through peremptory challenges. Further, during trials in which one of these eyewitness situations arises, attorneys can call expert witnesses to testify about the limitations of memory, which can potentially sensitize jurors to factors that predict better/worse eyewitness performance (Van Wallendael et al., 2007; Cutler et al., 1990). If erroneous juror beliefs can be corrected during trial, their impact may be reduced.

Limitations and future directions

The primary limitation of the current studies concerns the utilization of written trial simulations and undergraduate student participants. Simulation studies, particularly those relying on undergraduate students, are sometimes criticized for lacking in real-world consequentiality (Bornstein & McCabe, 2005; Vidmar, 2008). Such criticisms are especially a concern when courts and policy makers evaluate research findings (Monahan & Walker, 2005). However, reviews of mock jury research have demonstrated few systematic differences as a function of simulation verisimilitude (see, e.g. Bornstein, 1999; Bornstein & McCabe, 2005).

Other limitations include the fact that we did not include deliberation as part of the juror decision-making process, and the absence of a manipulation check in Study 1. The lack of a manipulation check limits the interpretations we can make about our findings. The fact that we used single items to measure juror attitudes for each of the three belief variables restricts our ability to calculate reliability coefficients. Although the measures were face valid, it is possible that our single items did not exactly tap into what we intended. A possible direction for future research is to develop a questionnaire to measure jurors' attitudes about these factors. General attitudes toward eyewitnesses are not strong predictors of jurors' decisions (Narby & Cutler, 1994), but it is possible that a measure focusing on more specific beliefs (i.e. about which factors do and do not influence eyewitness reliability) would have more predictive utility (Van Wallendael et al., 2007). A psychometrically sound attitude questionnaire could then be used in future studies, as well in trial consultation, to examine how various judgments might be related.

Future research should examine other ways in which jurors' beliefs predict their trial judgments. Further, the impact of interventions to reduce the effect of erroneous juror beliefs is needed. Will *voir dire* deselection reduce the number of misinformed jurors and lead to less misinformed juries overall? Can juries be educated during trial by the testimony of expert witnesses in such a way that erroneous beliefs can be modified before decisions are affected by them? The present studies show that laypeople's beliefs about what (and how) select factors influence eyewitness reliability vary, and that those beliefs predict their judgments at trial. Attorneys and the courts therefore need to take jurors' beliefs into account.

Note

1. Although mock jurors rated the credibility of several witnesses, we only report the eyewitness credibility ratings here because our focus is on perceptions of the eyewitness. Results on credibility of the other witnesses are available from the first author.

References

Abshire, J., & Bornstein, B.H. (2003). Juror sensitivity to the cross-race effect. *Law and Human Behavior*, 27, 471–480.

Baron, R.M., & Kenny, D.A. (1986). The moderator–mediator variable distinction in social psychological research: Conceptual, strategic, and statistical considerations. *Journal of Personality and Social Psychology*, 51, 1173–1182.

Bartlett, J.C., & Memon, A. (2007). Eyewitness memory in young and older adults. In R.C.L. Lindsay, D.F. Ross, J.D. Read, & M.P. Toglia (Eds.), *The handbook of eyewitness psychology (Vol. II): Memory for people* (pp. 309–338). Mahwah, NJ: Erlbaum.

Benton, T.R., Ross, D.F., Bradshaw, E., Thomas, W.N., & Bradshaw, G.S. (2006). Eyewitness memory is still not common sense: Comparing jurors, judges, and law enforcement to eyewitness experts. *Applied Cognitive Psychology*, 20, 115–130.

Bornstein, B.H. (1999). The ecological validity of jury simulations: Is the jury still out? *Law and Human Behavior*, 23, 75–91.

Bornstein, B.H., & McCabe, S.G. (2005). Jurors of the absurd? The role of consequentiality in jury simulation research. *Florida State University Law Review*, 32, 443–467. Retrieved from http://www.law.fsu.edu/journals/lawreview/downloads/322/Bornstein-McCabe.pdf

Bornstein, B.H., Zickafoose, D.J., & O'Bryant, S. (2008). Intuitions about arousal and eyewitness memory: Effects on mock jurors' judgments. *Law and Psychology Review*, 32, 109–129. Retrieved from http://heinonline.org

Bottoms, B.L., Golding, J.M., Stevenson, M.C., Wiley, T.R.A., & Yozwiak, J.A. (2007). A review of factors affecting jurors' decisions in child sexual abuse cases. In M.P. Toglia, J.D. Read, D.F. Ross, & R.C.L. Lindsay (Eds.), *Handbook of eyewitness psychology (Vol. I): Memory for events* (pp. 509–543). Mahwah, NJ: Erlbaum.

Cutler, B.L., Penrod, S.D. & Dexter, H.R. (1990). Juror sensitivity to eyewitness identification evidence. *Law and Human Behavior*, 14, 185–191.

Cutler, B.L., Penrod, S.D., & Stuve, T.E. (1988). Juror decision making in eyewitness identification cases. *Law and Human Behavior*, 12, 41–55.

Deffenbacher, K.A., & Loftus, E.F. (1982). Do jurors share a common understanding concerning eyewitness behavior? *Law and Human Behavior*, 6, 15–30.

Devenport, J.L., Penrod, S.D., & Cutler, B.L. (1997). Eyewitness identification evidence: Evaluating commonsense evaluations. *Psychology, Public Policy, and Law*, 3, 338–361.

Dunning, D., & Stern, L.B. (1994). Distinguishing accurate from inaccurate eyewitness identification via inquiries about decision processes. *Journal of Personality and Social Psychology*, 67, 818–835.

Golding, J.M., Dunlap, E., & Hodell, E.C. (2009). Jurors' perceptions of children's eyewitness testimony. In B.L. Bottoms, C.J. Najdowski, & G.S. Goodman (Eds.), *Children as victims, witnesses, and offenders: Psychological science and the law* (pp. 188–208). New York, NY: Guilford Press.

Holcomb, M.J. & Jacquin, K.M. (2007). Juror perceptions of child eyewitness testimony in a sexual abuse trial. *Journal of Child Sexual Abuse: Research, Treatment, & Program Innovations for Victims, Survivors, & Offenders*, 16, 79–95.

Kassin, S.M., & Barndollar, K.A. (1992). The psychology of eyewitness testimony: A comparison of experts and prospective jurors. *Journal of Applied Social Psychology*, 22, 1241–1249.

Kassin, S.M., Tubb, V.A., Hosch, H.M., & Memon, A. (2001). On the 'general acceptance' of eyewitness testimony research. *American Psychologist*, 56, 405–416.

Leippe, M.R., & Romanczyk, A. (1989). Reactions to child (versus adult) eyewitnesses: The influence of juror's preconceptions and witness behavior. *Law and Human Behavior*, 13, 103–132.

Leippe, M.R., Manion, A.P., & Romanczyk, A. (1992). Eyewitness persuasion: How and how well do fact finders judge the accuracy of adults' and children's memory reports? *Journal of Personality and Social Psychology*, 63, 181–197.

Lindsay, R.C.L. (1994). Expectations of eyewitness performance: Jurors' verdicts do not follow from their beliefs. In D.F. Ross, J.D. Read, & M.P. Toglia (Eds.), *Adult eyewitness testimony: Current trends and developments* (pp. 362–384). Cambridge, UK: Cambridge University Press.

Monahan, J., & Walker, L. (2005). *Social science in law* (6th ed). New York, NY: Foundation Press.

Mueller-Johnson, K. (2005). Older eyewitnesses: Eyewitness accuracy, suggestibility and the perception of credibility. *Dissertation Abstracts International*, 66, 2326.

Myers, J.E., Redlich, A., Goodman, G., Prizmich, L., & Imwinkelried, E. (1999). Jurors' perceptions of hearsay in child sexual abuse cases. *Psychology, Public Policy, & Law*, 5, 388–419.

Narby, D.J., & Cutler, B.L. (1994). Effectiveness of voir dire as a safeguard in eyewitness cases. *Journal of Applied Psychology*, 79, 724–729.

Newcombe, P.A. & Bransgrove, J. (2007). Perceptions of witness credibility: Variations across age. *Journal of Applied Developmental Psychology*, 28, 318–331.

Penrod, S.D., & Cutler, B.L. (1995). Witness confidence and witness accuracy: Assessing their Forensic relation. *Psychology, Public Policy, and Law*, 1, 817–845.

Pickel, K.L. (2007). Remembering and identifying menacing perpetrators: Exposure to violence and the weapon focus effect. In R.C.L. Lindsay, D.F. Ross, J.D. Read, & M.P. Toglia (Eds.), *The handbook of eyewitness psychology: Memory for people* (Vol. II, pp. 339–360). Mahwah, NJ: Erlbaum.

Poole, D.A., & White, L.T. (1991). Effects of question repetition on eyewitness testimony of children and adults. *Developmental Psychology*, 27, 975–986.

Pozzulo, J.D. & Dempsey, J.L. (2009). Witness factors and their influence on jurors' perceptions and verdicts. *Criminal Justice and Behavior*, 36, 923–934.

Pozzulo, J.D., Lemieux, J.M.T., Wells, E., & McCuaig, H.J. (2006). The influence of eyewitness identification decisions and age of witness on jurors' verdicts and perceptions of reliability. *Psychology, Crime, & Law*, 12, 641–652.

Pozzulo, J.D., & Lindsay, R.C.L. (1998). Identification accuracy of children versus adults: A meta-analysis. *Law and Human Behavior*, 22, 549–570.

Read, J.D. & Desmarais, S.L. (2009). Lay knowledge of eyewitness issues: A Canadian evaluation. *Applied Cognitive Psychology*, 23, 301–326.

Roebers, C.M., & Schneider, W. (2001). Memory for an observed event in the presence of prior misinformation: Developmental patterns of free recall and identification accuracy. *British Journal of Developmental Psychology*, 19, 507–524.

Ross, D.F., Dunning, D., Toglia, M.P., & Ceci, S. (1990). The child in the eyes of the jury: Assessing mock jurors' perceptions of the child witness. *Law and Human Behavior*, 14, 5–23.

Sauerland, M., & Sporer, S. (2009). Fast and confident: Postdicting eyewitness identification accuracy in a field study. *Journal of Experimental Psychology: Applied*, 15, 46–62.

Shaw, J.I., & Skolnick, P. (1994). Sex differences, weapon focus, and eyewitness reliability. *Journal of Social Psychology*, 134, 413–420.

Sobel, M.E. (1982). Asymptotic intervals for indirect effects in structural equations models. In S. Leinhart (Ed.), *Sociological methodology 1982* (pp. 290–312). San Francisco, CA: Jossey-Bass.

Sporer, S.L. (1993). Eyewitness identification accuracy, confidence, and decision times in simultaneous and sequential lineups. *Journal of Applied Psychology*, 78, 22–33.

Sporer, S.L. (1994). Decision-times and eyewitness identification accuracy in simultaneous and sequential lineups. In D.F. Ross, J.D. Read, & M.P. Toglia (Eds.), *Adult eyewitness testimony: Current trends and developments* (pp. 300–327). Cambridge, UK: Cambridge University Press.

Sporer, S.L., Penrod, S., Read, D., & Cutler, B. (1995). Choosing, confidence, and accuracy: A meta-analysis of the confidence–accuracy relation in eyewitness identification studies. *Psychological Bulletin*, 118, 315–327.

Steblay, N.M. (1992). A meta-analytic review of the weapon focus effect. *Law and Human Behavior*, 16, 413–424.

Van Wallendael, L.R., Cutler, B.L., Devenport, J., & Penrod, S. (2007). Mistaken identification = erroneous conviction? Assessing and improving legal safeguards. In R.C.L. Lindsay, D.F. Ross, J.D. Read, & M.P. Toglia (Eds.), *The handbook of eyewitness psychology. (Vol. II): Memory for people* (pp. 557–572). Mahwah, NJ: Erlbaum.

Vidmar, N. (2008). Civil juries in ecological context: Methodological implications for research. In B.H. Bornstein, R.L. Wiener, R. Schopp, & S.L. Willborn (Eds.), *Civil juries and civil justice: Psychological and legal perspectives* (pp. 35–65). New York, NY: Springer.

Minimization and maximization techniques: assessing the perceived consequences of confessing and confession diagnosticity

Allyson J. Horgan[a], Melissa B. Russano[b], Christian A. Meissner[a] and Jacqueline R. Evans[a]

[a]Department of Psychology, University of Texas at El Paso, El Paso, Texas, USA; [b]Roger Williams University, Bristol, Rhode Island, USA

Identifying interrogation strategies that minimize the likelihood of obtaining false information, without compromising the ability to elicit true information, is a challenge faced by both law enforcement and scientists. Previous research suggests that minimization and maximization techniques may be perceived by a suspect as an expectation of leniency and a threat of harsher punishment, respectively, and that these approaches may be associated with false confessions. The current studies examine whether it is possible to distinguish between minimization and maximization techniques that do or do not influence a suspect's perceptions of the consequences of confessing. Results indicate that techniques that manipulate the perceived consequences of confessing influence both the decision to confess and the diagnostic value of confession evidence.

Introduction

Increasing true confessions from the guilty and eliminating false confessions from the innocent are two important interests of the criminal justice system. Obtaining true confessions allows open cases to be closed quickly and promotes guilty pleas, speeding up the conviction process (Costanzo, 2004). The importance of reducing or eliminating false confessions has become evident given the role of (false) confession evidence in recent DNA exonerations (Kassin et al., 2010). The Innocence Project (www.innocenceproject.org) reports that approximately 25% of the over 250 wrongful conviction cases were the product of, at least in part, a false admission elicited from the defendant.

Although research has focused on the problem of false confessions and the various factors that may lead a person to falsely implicate themselves (Gudjonsson, 2003; Kassin et al., 2010), more recent studies have begun to explore the diagnostic value of confessions (or the ratio of true to false confessions elicited) resulting from various police interrogation techniques (see Meissner, Russano, & Narchet, 2010; Narchet, Meissner, & Russano, in press). We believe it is of critical importance to identify those techniques that maximize the diagnostic value of confession evidence, not just those that produce false confessions – particularly if we are to encourage the law enforcement community to seriously consider the results of social science research and adapt their procedures accordingly. Furthermore, we believe it imperative that such recommendations have a strong empirical basis, grounded in psychological theory and evaluated using appropriate experimental rigor (see Meissner, Hartwig, & Russano, 2010; Meissner, Russano, & Narchet, 2010).

The purpose of the current study was to further our understanding of the diagnostic value of confessions obtained using two common approaches to interrogation, namely minimization and maximization tactics. Previous research has indicated that these approaches (which actually each consist of a package of techniques) are associated with the elicitation of false confessions (Kassin & Kiechel, 1996; Kassin & McNall, 1991; Klaver, Lee, & Rose, 2008; Narchet et al., in press; Russano et al., 2005), suggesting perhaps that these approaches should be avoided. For reasons that will be discussed below, this advice may be impractical. The goal of the current study was to explore whether some forms of these common interrogative methods used by law enforcement might prove more diagnostic than others.

Kassin and McNall (1991) originally argued that most modern-day interrogation techniques can be identified as either a minimization or maximization technique. *Minimization* generally involves a gentle, friendly approach in which the interrogator attempts to gain the suspect's trust and minimize the seriousness of the offense. Examples of minimization techniques include stressing the importance of cooperation, expressing sympathy, blaming the victim, and providing face-saving excuses. *Maximization*, on the other hand, generally involves the use of harsher techniques or 'scare tactics' that are confrontational in nature and are designed to emphasize the seriousness of the situation. Examples of maximization techniques include expressing absolute certainty in the suspect's guilt, shutting down denials, exaggerating the seriousness of the offense, and bluffing about evidence. During an interrogation, an investigator may use multiple forms of minimization and/or maximization (cf. Leo, 1996). For example, an interrogator might tell a suspect that officers found his fingerprints on the murder weapon (a maximization technique), and then justify the crime by saying that the suspect must have been provoked by the victim (a minimization technique).

Previous research suggests that minimization and maximization techniques manipulate the suspect's perceptions of the consequences of confessing and are, therefore, often interpreted by the suspect as the equivalent of an expectation of leniency (if a confession is provided) or a threat of harsher punishment (if no confession is provided), respectively (Kassin & McNall, 1991). Kassin and McNall assessed participants' perceptions of various interrogation transcripts. When minimization techniques were displayed, such as excuses and justifications for the crime provided by the interrogator, participants perceived the interrogation as non-coercive, but believed that an implicit offer of leniency was made in return for the suspect's confession. The maximization transcript included the use of 'scare tactics' by the interrogator and an overstatement of the evidence against the suspect. Participants reading this transcript believed there was an implicit threat of harsher punishment if the suspect did not confess. Based upon these results, Kassin and McNall posited that the use of maximization and minimization techniques may alter a suspect's perception of the expected consequences of confessing, which may affect a suspect's decision to confess. Of course, it is particularly problematic if these techniques lower the diagnosticity of an interrogation by increasing the likelihood of false confession, and recent experimental works suggest that this is indeed the case (Kassin & Kiechel, 1996; Klaver, Lee, & Rose, 2008; Narchet et al., in press; Russano et al., 2005).

Russano et al. (2005) examined the use of minimization techniques versus an explicit offer of leniency during an interrogation using a novel laboratory paradigm. In the paradigm (which will be described in more detail in the method section), participants were induced to cheat (or not) during an experimental task. All participants were later subjected to an interrogation in which the experimenter accused them of cheating and asked them to confess to the act. In this interrogative context, Russano et al. found that the use of minimization techniques and an offer of leniency increased both true and false confessions. The researchers also examined diagnosticity, or the ratio of true to false confessions, finding that both minimization and direct offers of leniency decreased the diagnostic value of the interrogative evidence. Russano et al. also explored participants' perceptions of the interrogation and found that innocent participants exposed to minimization tactics felt more pressure to confess than those in the control condition. This paradigm has been used in subsequent studies to examine several other factors that impact interrogations and confessions such as investigator biases and the influence of non-coercive techniques (Meissner, Russano, & Narchet, 2010; Narchet et al., in press).

For example, Narchet et al. (in press) investigated whether an interrogator's pre-existing beliefs about the guilt or innocence of a suspect affects their interrogation strategy and the likelihood of eliciting true versus false confessions. In this study, interrogators were not scripted, but rather could apply any combination of 15 different interrogation techniques, including several forms of minimization and maximization. The researchers manipulated the guilt/innocence of the suspect, as well as the interrogators' expectations of guilt or innocence prior to the interrogation (by providing them with information regarding the likely guilt/innocence of participants). Narchet et al. found that the use of minimization and maximization techniques significantly reduced the diagnostic value of the interrogative evidence, and that this effect was exacerbated by interrogators' biases towards perceiving guilt or innocence. Minimization and maximization tactics also influenced participants' perceptions of the interrogation and thereby moderated the likelihood of obtaining true versus false confessions. Specifically, these techniques influence guilty participants' perceptions of proof and feelings of guilt, leading to increased true confessions in such cases. In contrast, minimization influenced innocent participants' perceptions of pressure to confess and therein increased the likelihood of false confessions. These findings are consistent with findings by Sigurdsson and Gudjonsson (1996) and Redlich and Kulish (2009) that true confessions appear to be the product of 'internal' pressures, while false confessions appear to be elicited via 'external' pressures.

Taken together, the implication of the previous research might be that police should avoid the use of minimization and maximization techniques. We believe it is unrealistic to think that law enforcement will be receptive to psychological research in this area if our efforts are focused solely on eliminating false confessions and encouraging the prohibition of various interrogative methods. Rather, we seek here to take a more positive approach in which we attempt to identify evidence-based approaches that might improve the diagnostic value of the confessions elicited – focusing here, in particular, on those methods that police use in their everyday practice (see Meissner, Hartwig, & Russano, 2010). To that end, the purpose of this study was to determine whether some minimization and maximization techniques might prove more diagnostic than others. We were interested in assessing whether only *some* of these techniques imply leniency or harsher punishment (thereby lowering diagnosticity by increasing false confession rates) and whether we might be able to distinguish between those techniques that do and do not imply consequences. Specifically, we theorized that minimization and maximization techniques can be divided into two types: those that appear to manipulate a suspect's perception of the consequences of confessing (i.e. leading the suspect to infer an offer of leniency or a threat of harsher punishment) and those that do not. It should be noted that the distinction between techniques that manipulate the perception of consequences and those that do not is a relative one, as individuals could still believe that certain consequences to confessing exist regardless of interrogation method. Table 1 provides examples of the minimization and maximization techniques used in the current set of studies that were hypothesized to vary the perceived consequences associated with confessing. These techniques were chosen based on the results of an initial pilot study in which participants were asked to sort examples of each technique based upon the degree to which they believed the consequences of confessing (or not) were manipulated.

We conducted a second pilot study to further assess the extent to which the proposed minimization and maximization techniques in Table 1 might manipulate

Table 1. Minimization and maximization techniques that vary and do not vary the perceived consequences of confession.

	Minimization	Maximization
Consequences	• stress benefit of cooperation • downplay consequences • face-saving excuses • minimize seriousness of offense	• exaggerate consequences • co-conspirators against each other
No consequences	• express sympathy • assume friendly demeanor • boost ego/use flattery • appeal to conscience	• assume unfriendly demeanor • firm belief in guilt

participants' perceptions of the consequences associated with confession. Ninety-five participants were recruited from the University of Texas at El Paso. Participants were asked to imagine themselves having been accused of committing a crime and finding themselves in an interrogation room. They were then asked to read through a series of statements that an investigator might relate to them in an interrogative context, and to rate their perceptions of the (implied) consequences associated with providing a confession based upon that statement using a scale from 1 = 'not harsh at all' to 7 = 'very harsh'. As minimization tactics are expected to reduce the perceived consequences associated with confession, we reverse coded these estimates to yield a measure of degree of 'manipulation.' Interrogative statements were generated for each of the approaches detailed in Table 1, and participants were randomly assigned to consider themselves either 'guilty' or 'innocent' of the crime for which they were being interviewed. A 2 (guilt vs innocence) × 2 (minimization vs maximization) × 2 (consequences vs no-consequences) mixed factorial ANOVA demonstrated significant main effects for guilt–innocence, $F(1,93) = 32.99$, $p < 0.001$, $\eta_p^2 = 0.26$, and manipulation of consequences, $F(1,93) = 7.26$, $p < 0.01$, $\eta_p^2 = 0.07$. No significant interactions were observed. As predicted, interrogative techniques believed to manipulate subjects' perception of the consequences associated with confession yielded significantly greater ratings ($Ms = 5.13$ vs 4.72, respectively). In addition, guilty participants perceived a greater degree of manipulation of consequences associated with confession than did innocent participants ($Ms = 5.98$ vs 3.86, respectively).

Based upon these pilot data, we conducted two studies examining individuals' perceptions of minimization and maximization tactics that were believed to manipulate perceptions of the expected consequences associated with confession (vs those that do not), and further to assess whether this distinction might also influence the diagnostic value of confessions elicited by guilty and innocent individuals. In Experiment 1, we examined the social perception of minimization and maximization techniques that do and do not manipulate the perception of consequences for the elicitation of confessions from others versus oneself. Previous survey research indicates that while participants believe that false confessions occur and that certain populations are vulnerable to providing them, they believe that they personally would never falsely confess (Henkel, Coffman, & Dailey, 2008). We wanted to further examine this finding using a design that asked participants to imagine themselves in an interrogation situation. In Experiment 2, we then examined how the use of interrogation techniques that manipulate the perceived consequences of confessing influence the likelihood of obtaining true versus false confessions in an experiential interrogative context (Russano et al., 2005). It was predicted that minimization and maximization techniques that influence the perceived consequences of confessing would elicit less diagnostic information and, in particular, increase the likelihood of a false confession. Based on previous research, it was also hypothesized that participants' perceptions of the interrogation (feelings of pressure, beliefs about the consequences associated with confessing, feelings of guilt, and perceptions of the proof against them) would be associated with participants' decision to confess (Narchet et al., in press).

Experiment 1
Method
Participants

One hundred and thirty-eight participants were recruited from undergraduate psychology courses at the University of Texas at El Paso. The sample was mostly Hispanic (74.6%) and female (60%), with a mean age of 24 years.

Design and procedure

A 2 (guilty vs innocent participant) × 2 (interrogation methods that manipulate consequences vs no consequences) × 2 (own vs other likelihood of confession) mixed factorial design was used in the present study. Guilt–innocence and interrogation method were manipulated between subjects, while participants' ratings of own vs other likelihood of confession were presented as a repeated measure.

Participants were presented with a description of the Russano et al. (2005) paradigm in which two students (A and B) were instructed to solve several logic problems, some of which were to be solved together and some individually. In the guilty condition, participants were told that during one of the individual problems, student A asked student B for help with one of the problems, and that student B responded by providing the answer. Participants in the innocent condition were told that the experimental session went according to the instructions given. In both conditions, participants read that after finishing the set of logic problems, the research assistant entered the testing room, explained that there seemed to be a problem, and separated students A and B. Participants then read an interrogation script in which the interrogation methods were manipulated. In the consequences condition, the research assistant (or 'interrogator') employed minimization and maximization techniques that were hypothesized to manipulate the perceived consequences of confessing. In the no manipulation of perceived consequences condition, the research assistant employed minimization and maximization techniques that were hypothesized not to manipulate the perceived consequences of confessing. Table 1 provides examples of each of the techniques used by the interrogator. At the end of both interrogation scenarios, the research assistant asked student B to sign a statement admitting to sharing information on the individual problem. After reading the introduction and interrogation scenario, participants estimated the probability (0–100% scale) that: (1) they would sign a confession statement if they were placed in that situation and (2) other people would sign a confession statement if they were placed in that situation.

Table 2. Rated probability of self vs others confessions as a function of interrogation method.

		Self	Others
Consequences	Guilty	0.50 (0.51)	0.69 (0.21)
	Innocent	0.09 (0.28)	0.64 (0.25)
No consequences	Guilty	0.26 (0.44)	0.60 (0.24)
	Innocent	0.06 (0.24)	0.47 (0.26)

Note: standard deviations are provided in parentheses.

Results and discussion

A 2 (guilty vs innocent participant) $\times$ 2 (interrogation methods that manipulate consequences vs no consequences) $\times$ 2 (own vs other likelihood of confession) mixed factorial ANOVA was conducted. Table 2 provides the mean estimates of confession across cells of the design. Main effects of own versus other confession estimates, $F(1,134) = 23.58$, $p < 0.001$, $\eta_p^2 = 0.15$, guilt–innocence, $F(1,134) = 104.13$, $p < 0.001$, $\eta_p^2 = 0.44$, and interrogation method, $F(1,134) = 10.75$, $p < 0.01$, $\eta_p^2 = 0.07$, were found. Participants who read a guilty script were more likely to endorse confession (across own vs other estimates) than did those who read an innocent script ($Ms = 0.51$ vs 0.32, respectively), and participants believed themselves less likely to confess than others in the same situation ($Ms = 0.23$ vs 0.60, respectively). Importantly, participants who read a script that was thought to manipulate the consequences associated with confession were significantly more likely to endorse confession when compared with those reading a script that was proposed not to manipulate perceived consequences ($Ms = 0.48$ vs 0.35, respectively).

In addition to the main effects, a significant guilt–innocence $\times$ own–other confession $\times$ interrogation method interaction was observed, $F(1,134) = 4.24$, $p < 0.05$, $\eta_p^2 = 0.03$. To assess this interaction, separate ANOVAs were conducted for each interrogation method. For the no manipulation of consequences script, main effects of guilt–innocence, $F(1,67) = 8.22$, $p < 0.01$, $\eta_p^2 = 0.11$, and own–other confessions, $F(1,67) = 62.0$, $p < 0.001$, $\eta_p^2 = 0.48$, were found. For the manipulation of consequences script, these main effects for guilt–innocence, $F(1,67) = 15.97$, $p < 0.001$, $\eta_p^2 = 0.19$, and own–other confession, $F(1,67) = 44.75$, $p < 0.001$, $\eta_p^2 = 0.40$, were found as well as a guilt–innocence $\times$ own–other confession interaction, $F(1,67) = 10.86$, $p < 0.01$, $\eta_p^2 = 0.14$. The data suggest participants believed that while guilty others would be more likely to confess than innocent others when the consequences associated with confessing were not manipulated, they believed that both guilty and innocent individuals would be equally likely to confess under conditions in which the consequences of confessing were manipulated. When considering whether they, themselves, would confess under these conditions, participants believed that, if guilty, they would be more likely to confess when the consequences were manipulated than compared with the no manipulation condition. If innocent, however, participants rated the likelihood of themselves confessing as low regardless of interrogation method.

Taken together, the results of Experiment 1 indicated that participants perceived the use of manipulative techniques in the interrogation scripts and understood that such techniques may lead (other) people to falsely confess. However, participants failed to recognize the impact of manipulative techniques when estimating their own confession decisions. This finding is consistent with prior research indicating that participants believe that false confessions occur and that people have certain vulnerabilities to false confessions, but that they themselves are relatively immune to such situations (Henkel, Coffman, & Dailey, 2008). It appears that participants may be falling victim to the fundamental attribution error (Ross, 1977) by failing to take into account situational factors, like manipulation of the perceived consequences of confessing, when evaluating their own behavior in the interrogation room. In contrast, they appear to be perceptive to situational factors when considering how other people would react to an interrogation. This finding may also be a result of actor–observer effects (Jones & Nisbett, 1972). When participants are in the role of the observer, they believe other people will not be able to overcome the manipulative interrogation techniques and will confess. However, when placed in the actor role, participants believe they will overcome the situational effects and not falsely confess. In Experiment 2, we moved from examining the social perception of interrogation techniques to examining the actual behavior of participants in an experiential interrogative context using the Russano et al. (2005) paradigm.

Experiment 2
Method
Participants

One hundred and thirty-two participants were recruited for the current experiment. Participants were mostly female (65.2%) and Hispanic (88.6%), with a mean age of 19 years.

Design and materials

Participants were randomly assigned to one of four experimental conditions based on a 2 (guilty vs innocent) × 2 (minimization and maximization techniques that manipulate perception of consequences vs minimization and maximization techniques that do not manipulate perception of consequences) between-participants factorial design.

The manipulation of perceived consequences interrogation script and the no manipulation of perceived consequences script each contained a total of six interrogation techniques; four minimization and two maximization techniques (see Table 1). At the end of the interrogation, participants were asked to sign a confession statement that indicated, 'I admit to sharing information on the triangle problem.'

After the interrogation phase, participants completed a debriefing questionnaire that included several items regarding their perceptions of the interrogation, including (a) the amount of pressure they felt was placed upon them by the interrogator, (b) their assessment of the consequences associated with confessing, (c) how guilty they were made to feel by the interrogator, (d) their perceptions of the proof of guilt against them, and (e) how severe participants perceived the consequences would be if they admitted to sharing (all seven-point Likert scales). These items were selected given that they were most predictive of confessions in previous research (see Narchet et al., in press).

Procedure

Two male and two female undergraduate research assistants were recruited to participate as experimenters/interrogators. All research assistants were trained extensively to ensure that the interview scripts were followed for each participant and that the procedure was identical for each participant. Interrogations were video recorded and assessed to ensure that experimenters adhered to the scripted manipulations.

The procedure was consistent to that of Russano et al. (2005). The beginning of the experimental session was consistent for all conditions. A female confederate and a participant arrived at the lab at the scheduled experiment time. The testing room was a small, bare room with no windows, similar to what may be used for interrogations in a police station. After obtaining informed consent, the experimenter explained that the purpose of the study was to examine individual versus group decision-making. Once the pair had completed a short rapport-building task, they began the problem-solving phase of the experiment. The experimenter explained that the individual problems were to be completed entirely individually, without any discussion about answers or strategies. The team problems were to be worked on together by sharing information about strategies and answers. Participants were reminded several times about the importance of working together on the team problems and working alone on the individual problems. This instruction served as the critical rule of the experiment.

In the guilty condition, while working on the last individual problem, the confederate feigned difficulty arriving at an answer. After waiting to ensure that the participant had answered the problem, she asked the participant what answer he/she calculated. This gave the participant the opportunity to break the rules of the experiment or 'cheat.' Participants that did not comply with the request for information in the guilty condition or that attempted to elicit information from the confederate in the innocent condition were excluded in the analysis ($n = 16$). In the innocent condition, the confederate did not attempt to elicit any information about the problem from the participant.

After the participant and confederate completed the problems and a filler questionnaire, the experimenter explained that he or she had looked over the packets and there appeared to be a problem (note that the experimenter did not actually review the problems in order to remain blind to the condition). The experimenter then asked the confederate to leave the room in order to speak to both of them individually. After five minutes of isolation, the experimenter began questioning the participant about breaking the rules of the experiment by sharing information on one of the individual problems. The experimenter stated that the supervising professor had been notified, and that the professor wanted the experimenter to document the situation. The experimenter also informed the participant that the professor was irritated about the situation and might consider this a case of academic dishonesty.

At this point in the questioning, the experimenter continued with one of the two interrogation approaches, either the manipulation of consequences script or the no manipulation of consequences script. At the end of each of the interrogation scripts, the experimenter asked the participant to sign a statement admitting their participation in the cheating incident. When participants signed the statement, the experimenter thanked them for their cooperation, asked for an explanation of their side of the story, and then exited the room, explaining that someone would be with the participant shortly. When participants refused to sign the statement, the experimenter then went through as many as two abbreviated versions of the script, repeating the same request using different phrases. For those participants who still refused to sign the statement, the experimenter thanked them for their time and exited the room.

Once the experimenter left the room, a lab manager immediately entered the testing room to begin debriefing the participant. The lab manager explained the true purpose and set up of the experiment, explained that the participant was not in any trouble, and that there was no angry professor to face. The main focus of the debriefing was to ensure that the participant understood why the use of deception was necessary and that the participant understood he/she was not in any trouble. Participants provided a self-report rating of how much pressure they felt to sign the confession statement on a scale from 1 to 7, and then completed the debriefing questionnaire described previously.

Results and discussion

Manipulation check

As previously described, the debriefing questionnaire assessed, among other items, how severe participants believed the consequences would be to admitting to sharing information on the triangle problem on a scale from 1 (extremely severe) to 7 (not at all severe). Participants in the consequences condition perceived that the consequences of admitting to sharing information would be less severe than those participants in the no manipulation of consequences condition ($Ms = 4.00$ vs 3.41, respectively), $t(130) = 1.96$, $p = 0.05$, $d = 0.34$, thereby confirming our successful manipulation of the perceived consequences of confessing.

True vs false confessions

A 2 (interrogation method: consequences vs no consequences) $\times 2$ (guilt vs innocence) $\times 2$ (interrogator gender: male vs female) hierarchical log–linear analysis was conducted on participants' decision to confess (sign vs no sign). While interrogator gender was included as a control variable, no main effects or interactions involving this variable were observed. Confession rates for guilty and innocent participants across the interrogation manipulation are presented in Table 3, along with diagnosticity ratios computed across the interrogation conditions.

Consistent with previous research (Narchet et al., in press; Russano et al., 2005), a significant main effect of guilt was found, $\chi^2(1) = 50.53$, $p < 0.001$, $L = 2.89$, such that guilty participants were more likely to confess (89.4%) than innocent participants (31.8%). This main effect, however, was qualified by a significant interrogation method $\times$ guilt–innocence interaction, $\chi^2(1) = 8.48$, $p < 0.01$. To assess this interaction, the effect of the two interrogation methods on guilty and innocent participants was investigated separately. Pairwise comparisons demonstrated that true confessions significantly *decreased* when the interrogators used techniques that manipulated the suspect's perception of consequences as compared to when

Table 3. True and false confession rates and diagnosticity ratio by interrogation method.

Condition	True confessions	False confessions	Diagnosticity ratio
Consequences	81.8% (27)	42.4% (14)	1.93
No consequences	97.0% (32)	21.2% (7)	4.58

Note: $N = 33$ for each cell. Frequencies are provided in parentheses.

interrogators used techniques that did not manipulate the perception of consequences, $\chi^2(1) = 4.50$, $p < 0.05$, $L = 1.96$. In addition, false confessions significantly
increased when techniques that manipulated perception of consequences were used
as compared with when techniques that did not manipulate the perceived consequences were used, $\chi^2(1) = 3.60$, $p = 0.05$, $L = 1.20$. It appears that manipulating the
perceived consequences of confessing in an interrogation context works to
elicit confessions by raising the expected consequences of not confessing but then
decreasing these consequences in exchange for a confession. The perceptual contrast
effect created by the process of ramping up the consequences and then providing
an incentive for confessing appears to have significantly increased the likelihood of
a false confession while reducing true confessions. In the next section, we further
examine the factors that influence the decision to confess for both innocent and guilty
participants.

Diagnosticity was computed as the ratio of true-to-false confessions elicited,
with higher ratios indicating a greater likelihood of true (versus false) evidence
being elicited in each interrogation condition. Consistent with the trade-off in
true versus false confessions across the interrogation manipulation noted above,
it appears that techniques that do not manipulate the perceived consequences
associated with confessing were 2.37 times more diagnostic than techniques that
manipulated participants' perceptions of the consequences.

Decision making in the interrogation room – predicting true vs false confessions

In order to investigate participants' decision making process, the debriefing
questionnaire assessed participant's perceptions of the interrogation, including: (a)
the amount of pressure they felt was placed upon them by the interrogator, (b) their
assessment of the consequences associated with confessing, (c) how guilty they were
made to feel by the interrogator, and (d) their perceptions of the proof of guilt
against them. Logistic regressions were conducted separately for guilty and innocent
participants to assess the associations between these measures and the likelihood of
true versus false confessions. Significant regression models were observed for both
guilty, $\chi^2(4) = 16.51$, $p < 0.01$, and innocent, $\chi^2(4) = 25.49$, $p < 0.001$, participants.
Results of the guilty model suggested that true confessions were significantly
associated with participants' feelings of guilt, $\beta = 0.75$, $Wald = 4.13$, $p < 0.05$, and
their perceptions of the proof of guilt, $\beta = 0.66$, $Wald = 4.15$, $p < 0.05$. In contrast,
the innocent model demonstrated that false confessions were significantly associated
with participants' perceptions of pressure, $\beta = 0.55$, $Wald = 6.44$, $p = 0.01$, and the
expected consequences associated with confessing, $\beta = 0.54$, $Wald = 8.39$, $p < 0.01$.
Overall, true confessions were more likely when participants experienced internal
pressure (feelings of guilt and perceptions of proof), while false confessions were
more likely when participants experienced external pressure (interrogative pressure
and severity of consequences).

General discussion

Previous research has found that the use of minimization and maximization
techniques in interrogations can manipulate a suspect's perceptions of the
consequences associated with confessing (Kassin & McNall, 1991). Given the

association of these techniques with false confessions and reduced diagnosticity of confession evidence (Narchet et al., in press; Russano et al., 2005), the current study sought to determine whether some minimization and maximization techniques might prove more diagnostic than others by investigating whether those techniques that manipulate the suspect's perception of the consequences of confession are lowering diagnosticity by increasing the false confession rate. Because minimization and maximization techniques represent the most pervasive techniques used by law enforcement, it was important to examine whether certain techniques might prove more diagnostic than others in order to provide evidence-based alternatives to law enforcement agencies.

Across two studies, the use of certain minimization and maximization techniques succeeded in manipulating the perceived consequences of confessing. This manipulation of perceived consequences influenced both participants' beliefs about whether they and others would confess (Experiment 1) and also influenced the diagnostic value of confession evidence elicited from participants (Experiment 2). Participants believed that other people would be more susceptible to falsely confessing when the expected consequences associated with confessing were manipulated, but did not believe this manipulation would influence their own decisions to confess if innocent. However, when actually engaging in an experiential interrogative context (Russano et al., 2005), participants were vulnerable to the manipulation of consequences and were thereby more likely to provide a false confession. A comparison of predicted (self) confession rates (Experiment 1) to actual confession rates (Experiment 2) reveals that while the pattern of likelihood of true and false confessions is similar, participants in Experiment 1 greatly underestimated the likelihood of confession. This suggests that participants underestimated the power of the interrogation context. Additionally, tactics that manipulate the perception of consequences proved less diagnostic, as they also reduced the likelihood of obtaining a true confession.

Our assessment of participants' decision processes suggested that the decision to confess was based on different mechanisms for guilty and innocent participants, and that this may have been related to the shifts in true and false confessions observed across our manipulation of interrogative approaches. Specifically, guilty participants were driven to confess based on the perceived amount of proof the interrogator had against them and how guilty they felt about their actions – factors that were emphasized to a greater extent in the 'no consequences' condition. In contrast, innocent participants were more influenced by their perception of the expected consequences of confession and the degree of pressure placed upon them to confess – factors that were exaggerated to a greater extent in the 'consequences' condition. Thus, it appears that the current manipulation of no consequences versus consequences techniques may have distinguished the placement of pressure on internal versus external mechanisms leading to variation in true versus false confessions, respectively (see also Narchet et al., in press; Redlich & Kulish, 2009). These findings suggest that techniques focusing on the strength of the (true) evidence against a suspect and emphasizing the morality of confession may be more productive for eliciting true confessions, limiting the vulnerability of the innocent and increasing the diagnostic value of the confession evidence.

We believe that further research should similarly seek to identify techniques that will increase the diagnostic value of confession evidence, and importantly those that reduce or eliminate the likelihood of eliciting a false confession. In this study we collapsed across minimization and maximization techniques that do and do not manipulate perception of consequence; it is possible, however, that minimization techniques that do not manipulate perception of consequences may be more diagnostic when used in isolation as compared to when these tactics are paired with maximization techniques. Moreover, there may be other important dimensions within minimization and maximization techniques (e.g. level of rapport established or tone of the interview) that researchers could further assess. It is important that we develop a better theoretical and practical understanding of these techniques, including the various psychological mechanisms (e.g. internal vs external sources of pressure) that result in true versus false confessions.

Given the importance of presenting diagnostic evidence in criminal trials and the significant costs associated with false confessions, there are practice and policy considerations that relate to the present findings. Under current US interrogative practice, all of the techniques tested in this study are legally permissible. Based on our findings, however, the continuing use of some of these techniques may be detrimental to the goal of eliciting true confessions while at the same time placing innocent persons at greater risk. Fortunately, based on the results of this study, for the first time we can now offer more precise recommendations about which minimization and maximization techniques might be best to avoid and which might be advocated. By avoiding the subset of techniques that manipulate the perception of consequences and increase 'external' pressure to confess (see Table 1), and focusing instead on other minimization and maximization techniques that place 'internal' pressure on suspects, law enforcement could significantly improve the diagnostic value of their interrogations. We encourage additional research along these lines, such that we might ultimately provide law enforcement with positive, evidence-based practices that will improve the outcomes of most interest to the criminal justice system (see Meissner, Hartwig, & Russano, 2010; Meissner, Russano, & Narchet, 2010; Narchet et al., in press).

The recent DNA exonerations have revealed the important role of false confession evidence in leading to wrongful conviction. Researchers have begun to examine factors that lead to false confessions and have found that the use of minimization and maximization techniques contribute to the false confession phenomenon (Kassin & McNall, 1991; Kassin & Kiechel, 1996; Klaver et al., 2008; Narchet et al., in press; Russano et al., 2005). The current studies were the first to directly distinguish between the various forms of minimization and maximization that are commonly used – separating those that do and do not manipulate a suspect's perception of the consequences associated with confession. Importantly, our studies found that such a distinction between minimization and maximization techniques can significantly influence the diagnostic value of interrogative evidence. Although these techniques do not eliminate the likelihood of eliciting a false confession, we believe that our results begin to provide an evidence-based perspective that could assist law enforcement in determining what really works in an interrogation room. We urge researchers to focus on identifying interrogative methods that improve the diagnostic value of confession evidence when designing future research studies.

Acknowledgement

The research reported in this paper was funded by the US Department of Defence and the National Science Foundation.

References

Costanzo, M. (2004). *Psychology applied to law.* Belmont, CA: Thompson/Wadsworth Learning.

Gudjonsson, G.H. (2003). *The psychology of interrogations and confessions: A handbook.* Chichester: John Wiley & Sons.

Henkel, L.A., Coffman, K.A.J., & Dailey, E.M. (2008). A survey of people's attitudes and beliefs about false confessions. *Behavioral Sciences & the Law, 26,* 555–584.

Jones, E.E., & Nisbett, R.E. (1972). The actor and observer: Divergent perceptions of the causes of behavior. In E.E. Jones, D.E. Kanouse, H.H. Kelley, R.E. Nisbett, S. Valins, & B. Weiner (Eds.), *Attribution: Perceiving the causes of behavior.* Morristown, NJ: General Learning Press.

Kassin, S.M., Drizin, S.A., Grisso, T., Gudjonsson, G.H., Leo, R.A., & Redlich, A.D. (2010). Police-induced confessions: Risk factors and recommendations. *Law & Human Behavior, 34,* 3–38.

Kassin, S.M., & Kiechel, K.L. (1996). The social psychology of false confessions: Compliance, internalization, and confabulation. *Psychological Science, 7,* 125–128.

Kassin, S.M., & McNall, K. (1991). Police interrogations and confessions: Communicating promises and threats by pragmatic implication. *Law & Human Behavior, 15,* 233–251.

Klaver, J.R., Lee, Z., & Rose, G. (2008). Effect of personality, interrogation techniques and plausibility in an experimental false confession paradigm. *Legal & Criminological Psychology, 13,* 71–88.

Leo, R.A. (1996). Inside the interrogation room. *Journal of Criminal Law & Criminology, 86,* 266–303.

Meissner, C.A., Hartwig, M., & Russano, M.B. (2010). The need for a positive psychological approach and collaborative effort for improving practice in the interrogation room. *Law & Human Behavior, 34,* 3–38.

Meissner, C.A., Russano, M.B., & Narchet, F.M. (2010). The importance of a laboratory science for improving the diagnostic value of confession evidence. In G.D. Lassiter & C. Meissner (Eds.), *Police interrogations and false confessions: Current research, practice, and policy recommendations.* Washington, DC: APA.

Narchet, F.M., Meissner, C.A., & Russano, M.B. (in press). Modeling the influence of investigator bias on the elicitation of true and false confessions. *Law & Human Behavior.*

Redlich, A.D., & Kulish, R. (2009, September). *True and false confessions: Self-reported experiences of offenders with serious mental illness.* Paper presented at the HUMINT: Integration of Science and Practice Conference, Ft Huachuca, AZ.

Ross, L. (1977). The intuitive psychologist and his shortcomings: Distortions in the attribution process. In L. Berkowitz (Ed.), *Advances in experimental social psychology.* New York, NY: Free Press.

Russano, M.B., Meissner, C.A., Narchet, F.M., & Kassin, S.M. (2005). Investigating true and false confessions within a novel experimental paradigm. *Psychological Science, 16,* 481–486.

Sigurdsson, J.F., & Gudjonsson, G.H. (1996). The relationship between types of claimed false confession made and the reasons why suspects confess to the police according to the Gudjonsson Confession Questionnaire (GCQ). *Legal & Criminological Psychology, 1,* 259–269.

Perceptions of sexual assault: expectancies regarding the emotional response of a rape victim over time

Marc A. Klippenstine[a] and Regina Schuller[b]

[a]East Central University, Ada, Oklahoma, USA; [b]York University, Toronto, Ontario, Canada

The present research examined how expectancies for a complainant's emotional response and the consistency of her emotional response over time impact perceptions of sexual assault. Participants ($N = 124$) were given one of four trial summaries in which the victim's emotional response (i.e. *tearful/upset, calm/controlled*) was varied at two points in time (i.e. *day following the alleged assault, during trial*). Similar to past findings, more support for the victim's claim was evidenced when she was portrayed as *tearful/upset* as opposed to *calm/controlled*, with participants' perceptions negatively influenced by emotional information that was incongruent with what would be considered typical of a sexual assault victim. Further analyses revealed, however, that emotions displayed at different points interacted to influence perceptions, with the consistently responding victim tending to receive more support for her claim than the victim who responded inconsistently over time. Mediation analyses revealed that the impact of the victim's emotional response on perceptions was mediated by the perceived typicality of her response. Implications of the research suggest, for both psychological and legal professionals alike, that it is incumbent upon those receiving information regarding a rape victim's emotional response to be more aware of its limited value and its potential prejudicial impact.

Introduction

Within the legal system, beliefs or expectancies about a crime can play a powerful role in guiding decision makers' (e.g. police, jurors, judges) evaluations and judgments of the alleged event. In the case of sexual assault, where corroborating evidence is often minimal and typically circumstantial and ambiguous (i.e. divergent account of what 'he said'/'she said'), it is perhaps not surprising that these expectancies can take on a significant role. Serving both a descriptive and a prescriptive function, they provide the decision maker with a simplified cognitive representation, or stereotype, of what a 'real' rape entails and how a 'genuine' victim of rape behaves (Bohner, 1998; Krahé, Temkin, & Bieneck, 2007).

In contrast to the narrow conception of rape that people typically hold, research consistently demonstrates that lay persons will question the validity of a sexual assault and judge the victim with greater skepticism, if the assault or those involved do not comport with their expectancies (e.g. Brown & Horvath, 2009; Du Mont,

Miller, & Myhr, 2003; Horney & Spohn, 1996; Horvath & Brown, 2009; Temkin & Krahé, 2008). Whether these belief structures touch upon victim and/or perpetrator behavior *prior to* (e.g. prior relationship; Schuller & Hastings, 2002), *during* (e.g. alcohol consumption; Hammock & Richardson, 1997; Schuller & Wall, 1998; Wall & Schuller, 2000), or *following* the alleged assault (e.g. emotional reaction; see generally, Bollingomo, Wessel, Sandvold, Eilertsen, & Magnussen, 2009), research has clearly demonstrated that expectancies regarding what typically occurs during a rape and what the 'appropriate' behavior of a sexual assault victim should be, powerfully guide the judgments of those evaluating her claim.

The present research focuses on one such set of expectancies – the victim's post-event behavior – that can take on particular significance in the adjudication of sexual assault. Given that victims are likely to testify at trial or make statements regarding the incident in a police interview, there is a potential for decision makers to use her emotion-related behavior, both verbal and non-verbal, to inform their evaluation of her claim (Kaufmann, Drevland, Wessel, Overskeid, & Magnussen, 2003). These expectancies can be particularly troubling given that lay beliefs regarding the crime of sexual assault are often squarely at odds with the body of data documenting the circumstances surrounding actual rape.

In this paper, we review the body of work examining decision makers' expectancies regarding the emotional reaction of a rape victim and investigate how these expectancies can impact their perceptions of her claim and the alleged assault. Past research has examined the *type* of emotional response expected of a rape victim but little research has examined expectancies regarding the *consistency* of the victim's emotions over time. As such, the present study builds upon this work and examines how expectancies regarding the consistency of the victim's response over time can impact perceptions of her claim. It is expected that victims who respond consistently, either in comparison to sexual assault victims in general or over time, should be considered more typical and therefore viewed as more believable. In contrast, an inconsistently responding victim will be viewed as atypical (i.e. not conforming to expectancies or the 'stereotypical' victim) and therefore will be viewed less favorably.

Expectancies regarding the sexual assault victim's emotional response

Research by Buddie and Miller (2001) explored participants' personal beliefs and cultural stereotypes about rape victims by asking them to generate a list of victim traits from either the perspective of their own personal beliefs or their perceptions of general cultural stereotypes regarding rape victims. Their results demonstrated that more rape myths were listed when generating cultural stereotypes, whilst partici-pants' personal beliefs were composed more of emotional (e.g. ashamed, hurt, angry) and behavioral reactions (e.g. crying) than rape myths. As well, women were found to be more likely than men to list these emotional and behavioral reactions as representing their personal beliefs about rape victims. The authors proposed that although an accurate perception of a rape victim involves an understanding that rape can be devastating and can result in a number of negative consequences, 'perceivers' understanding of the trauma of rape might not necessarily be beneficial for rape victims if that information is used to describe how rape victims *should* behave' (Buddie & Miller, 2001, p. 143).

In a similar vein, Burgess and Borgida (1999) suggested that prescriptive beliefs, or misconceptions about the emotional and behavioral reactions of rape victims, may represent stereotypes that can negatively influence people's expectancies and perceptions of a victim. Whereas expectancies regarding sexual assault have been traditionally captured by rape myth scales (e.g. Lonsway & Fitzgerald, 1994, 1995), Buddie and Miller (2001) suggested that these scales do not consider the victim's emotional and behavioral reaction as a part of the stereotype of rape victims. Indeed, such scales often suggest that rape is 'not' emotionally damaging to a rape victim and therefore do not produce a complete portrait of people's beliefs and expectancies about sexual assault.

Victims and observers may also rely on these 'emotional' expectancies when they are rendering decisions about whether the events constituted an 'actual' sexual assault (Peterson & Muehlenhard, 2004). For example, Kahn, Mathie, and Torgler (1994) demonstrated that women who did not acknowledge that they were sexually assaulted, despite the fact that the incident met the legal definition of sexual assault, were more likely to write rape scripts that involved strangers, aggression and violence, than were women who believed that they were assaulted. Extrapolating this to encompass expectancies regarding emotions, Kahn and Mathie (2000) suggested that victims might not label their experience as sexual assault if they did not experience a negative emotional reaction following the event. In support of this, Konradi (1999) found that sexual assault victims hold expectancies of the emotions that are typical of a sexual assault victim. For example, in her analysis of 32 semi-structured interviews with sexual assault survivors, Konradi (1999) found that survivors sought to produce an emotional demeanor consistent with the feeling 'rules' for both sexual assault victims and for witnesses in a court of law. Specifically, while 'victims perceived the courtroom to be a rational domain which called for a neutral, controlled, and polite demeanor' (Konradi, 1999, p. 55), they also believed that the demeanor of a real victim was consistent with someone who was damaged by the sexual assault.

The problem arises, however, when during a trial the defense attempts to discredit the victim's testimony on the grounds that her behavior and actions do not comply with the 'sexual and behavioral standards of the normative victim' (Larcombe, 2002, p. 131; see also, Matoesian, 1993). This includes highlighting any inconsistencies in her behavior, a factor that could include her emotional response following the assault. As such, a victim who responds inconsistently over time, even if some of that response corresponds to the expected emotional reaction of a sexual assault victim, may be believed to a lesser extent than one who responds in a consistent manner. The potential for an inconsistent emotional response is highly likely given that emotions have the potential to evolve over time in relation to a traumatic rape event (Frank & Anderson, 1987; Frazier, 1990; Frazier & Borgida, 1992; Meyer & Taylor, 1986). According to Matoesian (1993), it is this disjuncture between a victim's actual behavior and that expected of a 'real' victim that often influences blame assignment, with a victim who does not fit the 'ideal' victim being discredited and blamed more for what occurred. These findings are consistent with the existence of expectancies that define what is believed to be *typical* of a sexual assault incident, with those assaults that do not meet the criteria of this expectancy being deemed as less worthy of reporting or as less representative of a sexual assault. In short, such expectancies may provide another prejudicial factor that can disqualify a victim's claim in the eyes of the jurors.

Vignette research supports the existence of such expectancies. Specifically, research highlights the fact that calm, controlled, numbed, and/or unemotional victims, as compared to emotionally distraught victims, are less likely to be believed by outside observers (Ask & Landstrom, 2010; Baldry, 1996; Calhoun, Cann, Selby, & Magee, 1981; Hackett, Day, & Mohr, 2008; Krulewitz, 1982; Rodman, 1997; Winkel & Koppelaar, 1991). Applying these findings to legal situations suggests that expectancies regarding the victim's emotional response may negatively impact the legal evaluation of the alleged assault. Findings from research simulating a trial context confirm such an impact (Bollingomo, Wessel, Eilertsen, & Magnussen, 2008; Bollingomo et al., 2009; Golding, Fryman, Marsil, & Yozwiak, 2003; Kaufmann et al., 2003; Schuller, McKimmie, Masser, & Klippenstine; 2010; Vrij & Fisher, 1996; Wessel, Drevland, & Eilertsen, 2006). For example, using two testimony formats (i.e. written vs video) and varying the ambiguity of the testimony, Kaufmann et al. (2003) manipulated the victim's emotional display to be either congruent (e.g. showing despair with occasional sobs), neutral (e.g. in a flat, matter-of-fact manner), or incongruent (e.g. displaying positive and pleasant emotions) with what they determined were the expectancies of participants. Results confirmed past research and demonstrated that when a victim displayed congruent emotions she was rated as more credible, and the perpetrator was rated as more guilty, than when her emotions were incongruent, with the neutral condition falling between these two conditions. In replications of this study, researchers have demonstrated that lay persons (Bollingomo et al., 2009), as well as judges (Wessel et al., 2006) and police investigators (Bollingomo et al., 2008) were similarly impacted by the emotions expressed by the victim.

In an examination of the mechanism underlying these emotion-related effects, two recent studies have demonstrated a role for emotional expectancies. Research by Hackett et al. (2008) manipulated both the nonverbal and paralinguistic behavior of a rape victim to be emotionally expressive, numbed, or controlled. Results revealed that participants with a strong expectancy of an emotional response on behalf of the victim were more likely to view the victim as credible when she displayed the expected emotion as compared to when she was not emotionally expressive. The authors suggested that it may be expectancy violation rather than the victim's emotional response *per se* that biases perceptions of the victim. Similarly, manipulating the emotional demeanor of a rape victim to be emotional or neutral, Ask and Landstrom (2010) investigated the emotional victim effect on a sample of police trainees. Results revealed the usual effect with the emotional victim being regarded as more truthful in comparison to the neutrally responding victim. Analyses further revealed that it was indeed expectancies regarding the victim's response that mediated the effect of the victim's emotions on perceptions.

It is troubling to note that emotion-related effects occur despite the fact that the actual post-victimization demeanor of a victim can be quite variable. That is, many victims of rape may respond with a controlled and calm demeanor, often as a coping strategy (Petrak & Hedge, 2001). Indeed, research has demonstrated two basic responses to crime in general (see generally, Frieze, Hymer, & Greenberg, 1987; Wortman, 1983) and sexual assault specifically (Burgess & Holmstrom, 1974a, b, 1976, 1978; Winkel & Koppelaar, 1991): the *emotional victim* who displays distress clearly visible to others and the *numbed victim* whose emotions are in check and under control. As was noted by Winkel and Koppelaar, such findings suggest that 'the public's acquaintance with and awareness of self-presentation biases should be raised' (p. 37) and that those who come into contact with sexual assault victims (e.g. decision makers, counselors, & friends/families) should be made aware of the fact that victims will respond to the events in different ways, with no one particular manner of responding associated with a 'truthful' instance of sexual assault.

Present research

The purpose of the present study was to examine how information regarding the complainant's emotional display at trial impacts perceptions of the alleged sexual assault, and in particular how her demeanor at trial in light of her earlier emotional displays may impact the decision process. While past research has demonstrated that the emotional response of an alleged victim may be evaluated in terms of its correspondence to the expected emotional response of a typical victim, the present study examines whether the same effect may occur with respect to a complainant's pattern of responding over time. Indeed, research suggests that victims may not only be expected to be emotionally distraught but also to respond consistently over time (Larcombe, 2002). Given that such a comparison is likely to occur when the assessment of the assault occurs in the courtroom, where the victim's response may be evaluated for a second time, the present study used the context of a sexual assault trial to manipulate complainant emotional response both the *day following the incident* and then again *during her trial testimony*.

It was hypothesized, based on past research (e.g. Ask & Landstrom, 2010; Hackett et al., 2008; Kaufmann et al., 2003), that the complainant's claim of sexual assault would be believed more when she was portrayed as *tearful/upset* as opposed to *calm/controlled*. Moreover, given the potential problems that may arise when a victim's emotional response to a sexual assault incident changes over time (Larcombe, 2002), the extent that her emotional response at two points in time would interact to impact perceptions of the alleged assault was examined. While past research has not examined the impact of the victim's emotions at multiple points in time, it was expected that a complainant who responded consistently over time, regardless if that response was *tearful/upset* or *calm/controlled*, would be more likely to be believed than a complainant who responded inconsistently (Larcombe, 2002; see generally, Orvis, Cunningham, & Kelley, 1975).

Method

Participants and procedure

One hundred and twenty-four participants (67 women; 57 men; Mean age = 19.87, SD = 2.19) were recruited from various locations around a mid-western Canadian university campus. This resulted in approximately 15 men and 17 women per condition and all participants were classified as jury eligible (i.e. 18 years of age). Participants were asked to take part in a study examining jury decision making and were recruited through in-class requests and by approaching students in 'hang-out' locations around campus (e.g. cafeteria). Each participant received a stimulus packet that contained a trial summary, the dependent measures, and an initial instruction sheet that, among other things, asked them to assume the role of a real juror. The study required approximately 30 minutes to complete and participants received compensation in the form of entry in a $50 lottery. The sample was predominately upper middle (42.1%) or middle (46.3%) class and White (86.9%), with other classifications including 2.5% South Asian, 6.6% as Asian, 1.6% as Native, 0.8% as Black, and 1.6% as Other.

Materials

The 10-page trial summary involved a charge of sexual assault and included all aspects of an actual trial (i.e. opening statements and closing arguments, direct and cross examinations of all witnesses, judicial instructions). All information was presented in a narrative form and included testimony from the victim, her roommate, and examining physician, followed by the testimony of the alleged perpetrator. Within the summary, the emotional reaction of the complainant (i.e. *tearful/upset* or *calm/controlled*) was varied both the *day following the incident* and *during her trial testimony* to produce four versions of the trial summary. Specifically, the complainant's emotional response was manipulated in the trial testimony of both the complainant and her roommate, who testified regarding the complainant's reactions the day following the alleged assault. In general, the *tearful/upset* complainant was described as sobbing with a trembling voice, while the *calm/controlled* complainant was described as showing little emotion, remaining calm, and being composed and collected.

Dependent measures

Unless otherwise stated, all dependent measures were assessed using seven-point scales with the endpoints defined by either the wording of the item (e.g. 'not at all forced' to 'strongly forced') or participants' degree of endorsement (e.g. 'not at all likely' to 'very likely').

Guilt assessment

Participants first rendered a verdict (guilty, not guilty) and rated their degree of confidence in this decision. These measures were examined separately as well as combined to form a continuous scalar measure of assessment of guilt that ranged from −7 (complete confidence in a guilty verdict) to +7 (complete confidence in a not guilty verdict). Participants also rated the extent to which the events constituted sexual assault.

Case judgments

Participants' opinions concerning various aspects of the scenario were examined along several dimensions. For each target, three items (i.e. credibility, truthfulness, believability) were summed and averaged to create a composite measure of target credibility (αs = 0.82 and 0.85, for complainant and accused, respectively). Two items (i.e. blame, responsibility) were combined to create a composite measure of target *blameworthiness* (αs $= 0.72$ and 0.80, for complainant and accused, respectively). Five items were combined to form a composite measure of the *complainant's claim of non-consent*, with higher scores reflecting a greater belief in her claim (e.g. strength of her resistance, consensual nature of the sexual activity; $\alpha = 0.89$). And lastly, three items (e.g. his honest belief in her willingness, misinterpretation of her interest), were combined to form a composite measure of the *accused's mistaken belief in the complainant's consent* ($\alpha = 0.70$).

Complainant's emotional typicality

Seven items assessed the degree and nature of the complainant's emotional response the day following the incident and during her trial testimony (i.e. response was similar to that of a typical rape victim, unusualness of response (reverse coded), responded as expected, demeanor characterized a woman who was raped, response was understandable, response was believable, reaction was reasonable). Specifically, the *complainant's emotional typicality* was assessed for both '*the day following the incident*' ($\alpha = 0.93$) and '*during the trial testimony*' ($\alpha = 0.94$) with higher scores reflecting a more typical response.

Manipulation checks

Participants were asked to rate the complainant's emotional reaction both the *day following* the alleged sexual assault and *during her trial testimony* (i.e. not at all emotional to very emotional).

Results

Unless otherwise stated, all results discussed involve the results of 2 (victim's emotional response the day following: *tearful/upset, calm/controlled*), by 2 (victim's emotional response at trial: *tearful/upset, calm/controlled*), by 2 (gender of participant: male, female) ANOVAs. All interactions were further assessed using *post hoc* simple interaction and simple effect analyses.

Manipulation checks

Analyses revealed a number of emotion-related main effects, with the *tearful/upset* complainant, as compared to her *calm/controlled* counterpart being viewed as more emotional both the *day following* (Ms $= 4.41$ and 2.28, SDs $= 1.61$ and 1.35, $F(1,116) = 61.96, p = 0.001, \eta^2 = 0.35$) and *during trial* (Ms $= 5.08$ and 2.62, SDs $= 1.63$ and 1.59, $F(1,116) = 69.95, p = 0.001, \eta^2 = 0.38$).

Complainant emotional typicality

Main effects were found for both complainant emotional typicality the *day following the assault* ($F(1,116) = 18.67, p = 0.001, \eta^2 = 0.14$) and *during her trial testimony* ($F(1,114) = 19.52, p = 0.001, \eta^2 = 0.15$). The *day following the assault* the victim was rated as having an emotional response that was more typical of a sexual assault victim when she was *tearful/upset* ($M = 4.21$, SD $= 1.46$) as compared to *calm/controlled* ($M = 3.09$, SD $= 1.38$). A similar pattern was found for the victim's emotion *during trial* (Ms $= 4.69$ and 3.52; SDs $= 1.34$ and 1.51, for *tearful/upset* and *calm/controlled*, respectively). These main effects were not qualified by any interactions.

Guilt assessment

Verdict and assessment of guilt

A multiway frequency analysis was conducted to develop a logit model in which verdict (guilty, not guilty) was treated as the dependent variable and the remaining variables were treated as predictors. This analysis resulted in a model with a first-order effect of verdict with participants more likely to render a verdict of not guilty (76.6%) as compared to guilty (23.4%). This was qualified, however, by a three-way association between verdict and complainant emotional response the day following the assault as well as at trial. The model had a good fit between observed and expected frequencies, likelihood ratio G^2 ($N = 124$) $= 4.23$, d.f. $= 8$, $p = 0.84$. Results revealed that more guilty verdicts were rendered by participants when the complainant responded in a consistent manner (i.e. either *tearful/upset* or *calm/controlled* at both points in time). Specifically, when the complainant was *tearful/upset* the following day, participants were more likely to render guilty verdicts when she was also *tearful/upset* (70.6%) at trial during her trial testimony, as opposed to *calm/controlled* (29.4%). Alternatively, when the complainant was *calm/controlled* the day following participants were more likely to render guilty verdicts when the complainant was also *calm/controlled* (75%), as compared to *tearful/upset* (25%), during her trial testimony.

As for participants' assessment of guilt, results revealed an interaction involving complainant emotional response the day following the alleged assault and complainant emotional response at trial, $F(1,116) = 7.08$, $p < 0.009$, $\eta^2 = 0.06$. Supporting the findings above, simple main effect analyses revealed that, when the complainant was *tearful/upset* the day following the incident, the perpetrator was assessed as more guilty when the complainant was also *tearful/upset* ($M = 0.76$, SD $= 5.48$) at trial, as compared to when she was *calm/controlled* ($M = 3.44$, SD $= 4.03$), $F(1,120) = 4.50$, $p = 0.036$, $\eta^2 = 0.07$.

Events constitute sexual assault

In support of the above findings, analyses conducted on this single item similarly revealed an interaction of complainant emotional response the day following and complainant emotional response at trial, $F(1,116) = 7.95$, $p = 0.006$, $\eta^2 = 0.06$, with this interaction qualified by a three-way interaction involving gender of participant, $F(1,116) = 6.92$, $p = 0.01$, $\eta^2 = 0.06$. Analyses revealed that men, $F(1,116) = 13.72$, $p = 0.001$, $\eta^2 = 0.13$, were more likely to believe that the events constituted sexual assault when the complainant was *tearful/upset* the day following and also *tearful/upset* ($M = 4.62$, SD $= 1.98$) during her trial testimony, as compared to when she was *calm/controlled* during her trial testimony ($M = 2.23$, SD $= 1.30$), $F(1,116) = 10.74$, $p = 0.001$, $\eta^2 = 0.09$. Results revealed no significant effects for women.

Case judgments

Analyses revealed a number of significant two-way interactions involving the complainant's emotional response at both points in time (see Table 1 for means and univariate Fs). Simple main effects revealed that when the complainant was *tearful/upset* the day following the assault, participants were more likely to believe her claim of rape when she was also *tearful/upset* during her trial testimony, as compared to when she was *calm/controlled* at trial. Specifically, the complainant's

Table 1. Univariate Fs and means for the two- and three-way interactions involving gender of participant and complainant emotional response both the day following and at trial.

Judgments			Emotion the Following day	Emotion at trial		
				Tearful/Upset	*Calm/Controlled*	Fs (η^2)
Complainant's						
	Claim of non-consent		tearful/ upset	3.62 (1.22)	2.99 (1.15)*	6.52* (0.05)
			calm/ controlled	2.75 (1.05)	3.21 (1.33)	
		Women	tearful/ upset	3.73 (1.18)	3.41 (1.34)	4.13* (0.03)
			calm/ controlled	3.04 (1.15)	2.94 (1.37)	
		Men	tearful/ upset	3.51 (1.32)	2.56 (0.68)*	
			calm/ controlled	2.47 (0.87)	3.47 (1.26)*	
Accused's						
	Credibility		tearful/ upset	4.35 (1.40)	5.04 (1.19)*	5.33* (0.04)
			calm/ controlled	5.01 (1.00)	4.66 (1.35)	
		Women	tearful/ upset	4.46 (1.48)	4.71 (1.26)	4.62* (0.04)
			calm/ controlled	4. 77 (0.91)	4. 94 (1.14)	
		Men	tearful/ upset	4.23 (1.33)	5.36 (1.05)*	
			calm/ controlled	5.24 (1.06)	4.38 (1.53)*	
	Mistaken belief in consent		tearful/ upset	5.22 (1.24)	5.84 (0.97)*	5.31* (0.04)
			calm/ controlled	5.76 (0.77)	5.51 (1.06)	

Notes: For the univariate Fs, *$p < 0.05$; **$p < 0.01$; ***$p < 0.001$. For the means, based on simple effect analyses within each row, *significantly different from the *tearful/upset* condition ($p \leq 0.05$).

claim of non-consent was more believable, $F(1,120) = 4.00$, $p = 0.048$, $\eta^2 = 0.07$, while the accused was rated as less credible, $F(1,120) = 3.96$, $p = 0.049$, $\eta^2 = 0.07$, and as less likely to harbor a mistaken belief in the complainant's consent, $F(1,120) = 4.99$, $p = 0.027$, $\eta^2 = 0.07$.

Two of these interactions were qualified by a three-way interaction involving gender of participant (see Table 1). *Post hoc* simple interactions, and subsequent simple effects, revealed that for two of the above measures (complainant's claim of non-consent, $F(1,116) = 9.71$, $p = 0.002$, $\eta^2 = 0.18$; accused's credibility, $F(1,116) = 9.18$, $p = 0.003$, $\eta^2 = 0.19$) the pattern of results was significant again only for men. In both cases, men were significantly more favorable of the complainant's claim when the she responded consistently (either *tearful/upset* or *calm/controlled* at both points in time).

Mediational role of emotion-related expectancies

The current study assessed a 'snapshot' of the complainant's emotional typicality at two points in time. As such, it was decided to assess whether one of these measures of typicality (i.e. complainant's emotional typicality the *day following the assault*) would mediate the impact of the complainant's emotions at that one point in time (i.e. complainant's actual emotional response the *day following the assault*) on perceptions of the case, while holding the complainant's emotional response at the other point in time constant (i.e. *during her trial testimony*). Although the mediation analyses could be performed at either point in time, it was determined that holding the complainant's emotions *during her trial testimony* constant and assessing mediation of her emotions the *day following* would better capture the order in which participants were exposed to her emotions during the study.[1] Analyses revealed that, when the complainant's emotional response was held constant *during her trial* testimony to be *tearful/upset*, her emotional response the *day following* impacted the mediator and the mediator impacted perceptions (i.e. steps 2 and 3). As would be predicted by past research (Ask & Landstrom, 2010), at Step 4, the typicality measure was found to mediate the impact of the complainant's emotional response on perceptions of the complainant's credibility and claim of non-consent, the perpetrator's credibility and blame, and their overall assessment of guilt and the extent to which the events constituted sexual assault. In these cases, *post hoc* Sobel tests revealed that the mediator significantly reduced the impact of the complainant's actual emotional response on all of these measures (see Table 2). The initial conditions for mediation (i.e. Step 1), were not met when the complainant's emotional response was held constant *during her trial* testimony to be *calm/controlled*.

Discussion and conclusion

Results of the present research illustrate that a sexual assault victim's emotional response is but one of the factors that can influence participants' assessment of the alleged sexual assault. It seems that displays of emotion at different points in time (i.e. immediately following the event, during trial testimony) can interact to influence perceptions of the complainant, the perpetrator, and the event. Indeed, it appears that emotional consistency on the part of the complainant had a powerful influence

Table 2. Typicality of complainant response (day following) as a mediator for VER (day following) on case judgments when the complaint was *tearful/upset* during her trial testimony.

Mediation step		Unstandardized β	SE	t	p	Sobel
Step 1: Impact of the VER (day following) on participant perceptions						
Complainant credibility		−0.782	0.342	−2.29	0.026*	
Complainant's claim of non-consent		−0.869	0.287	−3.03	0.004*	
Perpetrator credibility		0.624	0.305	2.04	0.045*	
Perpetrator blame		−0.881	0.343	−2.57	0.013*	
Constitutes sexual assault		−1.14	0.460	−2.47	0.017*	
Assessment of guilt		3.16	1.15	2.75	0.008*	
Step 2: Impact of the VER (day following) on the mediator (i.e. typicality of the complainant's response day following)						
		−1.35	0.343	−3.94	0.000*	
Step 3: Impact of mediator (i.e. complainant emotional typicality day following) on perceptions						
Complainant credibility		0.596	0.091	6.55	0.000*	
Complainant's claim of non-consent		0.473	0.083	5.72	0.000*	
Perpetrator credibility		−0.389	0.093	−4.20	0.000*	
Perpetrator blame		0.551	0.097	5.67	0.000*	
Constitutes sexual assault		0.636	0.139	4.59	0.000*	
Assessment of guilt		−1.68	0.344	−4.89	0.000*	
Step 4: Impact of VER (day following) on perceptions when mediator included (i.e. complainant emotional typicality day following).						
Complainant credibility	CERF &	0.003	0.308	0.09	0.925	
	mediator	0.600	0.103	5.84	0.000*	−3.31**
Complainant's claim of non-consent	CERF &	−0.289	0.278	−1.04	0.303	
	mediator	0.429	0.092	4.64	0.000*	−3.05**
Perpetrator credibility	CERF &	0.123	0.313	0.394	0.695	
	mediator	−0.370	0.104	3.55	0.001*	2.71**
Perpetrator blame	CERF &	−0.171	0.329	−0.52	0.605	
	mediator	0.525	0.110	4.80	0.000*	−3.06**
Constitutes sexual assault	CERF &	−0.346	0.468	−0.739	0.463	
	mediator	0.584	0.156	3.75	0.000*	−2.68**
Assessment of guilt	CERF &	1.11	1.16	0.96	0.339	
	mediator	−1.52	0.385	−3.94	0.000*	2.78**

Note: *entry that significantly meets conditions/steps of mediation. Sobel test significant at *$p < 0.05$; **$p < 0.01$.

on participants', particularly men's, perceptions of the sexual assault. Specifically, participants were more likely to be supportive of the complainant's claim (i.e. her credibility, the claim of non-consent) and less supportive of the accused (i.e. his credibility, blame, mistaken belief claim, and assigning him more guilt) when the complainant's response was consistent over time, regardless of whether that response was *tearful/upset* or *calm/controlled*.

Furthermore, perceptions of the complainant's emotional typicality mediated the impact of the complainant's emotional response on participants' perceptions, particularly those of men. The impact of mediation was only found, however, when the first emotion presented to participants was perceived as typical (i.e. *tearful/ upset*). When the first emotion presented was perceived as atypical (i.e. *calm/ controlled*) no mediation was found and it was the presence of consistency that tended to result in greater support for the complainant's claim. Such results further the finding that it is more than general expectancies that influence participants' perceptions, but rather it is the application of these expectancies to the complainant in question, with both typicality and past behavior being important factors in the determination of impact. Such findings support past research (Ask & Landstrom, 2010; Hackett et al., 2008), which has also demonstrated a mediational role for expectancies regarding the victim's emotional response. Alternatively, these results may have stemmed from the fact that only a 'snapshot' of typicality was investigated and no measure of overall typicality was included.

Taken together these findings suggest that an individual's perceptions of an alleged sexual assault victim are based to some extent on the 'manner in which she gave the testimony' rather than completely 'on the factual content of what she said' (Kaufmann et al., 2003, p. 25). Participants appeared to judge the victim against an 'ideal victim stereotype' that involved an expectancy of emotional trauma. Moreover, when information about the victim's past emotional behavior was available, it appears that this additional information played a secondary role in developing expectancies regarding how the victim should be responding emotionally over time. These findings expand past research by demonstrating that it is not merely the type of emotional response displayed by sexual assault victims that influences perceptions of her claim but also the pattern of her multiple responses over time. Indeed, while past research has demonstrated that the victim's emotional demeanor influences perceptions of her claim (Bollingomo et al., 2008, 2009; Golding et al., 2003; Kaufmann et al., 2003; Vrij & Fisher; 1996; Wessel et al., 2006), the present research suggests that the victim's current emotional demeanor may also be evaluated in light of her prior emotional displays.

Implications

The implications of such findings are far reaching and, as suggested by past research, include all levels of the criminal justice system (i.e. police officers, counselors, attorneys, jurors, and judges; see generally Bollingomo et al., 2009). Consistency of the victim's response becomes particularly important when one considers that it is highly probable that the victim will have multiple opportunities to display an emotional response as she is processed through the legal system. Research has already demonstrated that the victim's emotional demeanor can influence legal decision makers at various levels of the system (Bollingomo et al., 2008, 2009; Golding et al., 2003; Kaufmann et al., 2003; Vrij & Fisher; 1996; Wessel et al., 2006). When you consider the fact that emotions have the potential to evolve over time (Frank & Anderson, 1987; Frazier, 1990; Frazier & Borgida, 1992; Meyer & Taylor, 1986), and the role that consistency of response may play in the legal evaluation of a complainant's claim, it becomes clear that the outlook is grim for a victim who responds in an unexpected fashion. Research has demonstrated that the type, frequency, and coping timeline of an emotional response does vary considerably from victim to victim (Frazier, 1990; Wyatt, Notgrass, & Newcomb, 1990), with complex combinations of internal (e.g. style of coping) and external factors (e.g. social support, severity of assault) influencing the victim's reaction (see generally, Fanflick, 2007). The findings of the present study therefore suggest that a victim who, through time or counseling, improves their ability to cope with the assault may be at a disadvantage given the expectancy of emotional consistency.

Within the legal system, potential prejudices can be dealt with in a variety of ways including judicial instructions, introduction of expert testimony regarding the nature of a sexual assault victim's emotional response, and through attorney and judicial closing remarks. It remains for future research to determine whether these methods would successfully curb the prejudicial nature of this information, with some research suggesting that the negative impact of this information can be lessened (e.g. Bollingomo et al., 2009; Ellison & Munro, 2009). As it may be difficult to prevent emotional information from being displayed, it is incumbent on the legal system that those receiving this information be more informed about its informational value and its potential prejudicial impact.

Limitations and directions for future research

In closing, several caveats of the present study must be noted. While the study employed a realistic trial simulation, participants were exposed to a summary only and were not required to take part in juror deliberations. Similarly, only a written depiction of the victim's emotional response during the trial was provided. Given that previous research on victim emotions (e.g. Kaufmann et al., 2003; Bollingomo et al., 2008, 2009) has found similar effects when a video format was used, it is likely that similar if not stronger effects would emerge when participants are presented with the visual depiction of a victim. In addition, participants in the current study represent a rather homogeneous (i.e. well educated, middle class) group of eligible jurors, and it remains an empirical question as to whether a more heterogeneous sample would yield similar findings. It is possible, however, that participants' age and education level may actually render them less accepting of rape myths and expectancies, and therefore effects with this sample may be muted. In addition, to further examine the complicated role that victim emotion may play in trials of sexual assault, future research will need to investigate the role of other factors such as the length of time between the various responses of the victim and perhaps to whom she discloses the account. That is, if participants have an expectancy of a negative emotional response on the part of the victim, is there a point in time at which that expectancy ceases? Given the variability in emotional responses that are possible, it is left for future research to address the issue of just how different types of emotions (e.g. anger, hatred, depression) on the part of the victim can impact perceptions of the sexual assault. Similarly, the present research only examined the role of expectancies regarding a female victim, given that men are also victims of sexual assault future research will need to explore the implications of emotional expectancies regarding this population of victims.

Much of the research examining the impact of the emotional demeanor of a sexual assault victim has been conducted at the time of the trial. It is clear from the present research that this static approach fails to capture the fact that information raised in a trial about past demeanor will interact with information about the current demeanor of the victim. Unfortunately, it appears that mock jurors not only prefer a stereotypical demeanor, but also consistency in this demeanor over time, thus denying the realistic possibility that a victim of sexual assault may be labile in her emotional reactions and unable to present a consistent image.

Note

1. This order represents the presentation that would take place during an actual courtroom situation, where the complainant would tell her story first followed by the retelling of the events by any witnesses (e.g. her roommate). Mediation analyses based on the chronological order that the victim's emotions occurred during the events revealed results that were similar to those reported. These results were considered redundant and therefore were not reported.

References

Ask, K., & Landstrom, S. (2010). Why emotions matter: Expectancy violations and affective response mediate the emotional victim effect. *Law and Human Behavior, 34*, 392–401.

Baldry, A.C. (1996). Rape victims' risk of secondary victimization by police officers. *Issues in Criminological and Legal Psychology, 25*, 65–68.

Bohner, G. (1998). *Rape myths: Social psychological studies on attitudes that exonerate the assailant and blame the victim of sexual violence*. Landau, Germany: Verlag Empirische Padogogik.

Bollingomo, G.C., Wessel, E.O., Eilertsen, D.E., & Magnussen, S. (2008). Credibility of the emotional witness: A study of ratings by police investigators. *Psychology, Crime & Law, 14*, 29–40.

Bollingomo, G.C., Wessel, E.O., Sandvold, Y., Eilertsen, D.E., & Magnussen, S. (2009). The effect of biased and non-biased information on judgments of witness credibility. *Psychology, Crime & Law, 15*, 61–71.

Brown, J., & Horvath, M. (2009). Do you believe her and is it real rape? In M. Horvath & J. Brown (Eds.), *Rape: Challenging Contemporary Thinking* (pp. 325–342). Portland, Oregon: Willan Publishing.

Buddie, A.M., & Miller, A.G. (2001). Beyond rape myths: A more complex view of perceptions of rape victims. *Sex Role, 45*, 139–160.

Burgess, A.W., & Holmstrom, L.L. (1974a). Rape trauma syndrome. *American Journal of Psychiatry, 131*, 981–985.

Burgess, A.W., & Holmstrom, L.L. (1974b). *Rape: Victims of crisis*. Bowie, MD: Brady.

Burgess, A.W., & Holmstrom, L.L. (1976). Coping behavior of the rape victim. *American Journal of Psychiatry, 133*, 413–418.

Burgess, A.W., & Holmstrom, L.L. (1978). Recovery from rape and prior life stresses. *Research in Nursing and Health, 1*, 165–174.

Burgess, D., & Borgida, E. (1999). Who woman are, who woman should be: Descriptive and prescriptive gender stereotyping in sex discrimination. *Psychology, Public Policy and Law, 5*, 665–692.

Calhoun, L.G., Cann, A., Selby, J.W., & Magee, D.L. (1981). Victim emotional response: Effects on social reaction to victims of rape. *British Journal of Social Psychology, 20*, 17–21.

Du Mont, J., Miller, K. & Myhr, T.L. (2003). The role of 'real rape' and 'real victim' stereotypes in the police reporting practices of sexually assaulted women. *Violence Against Women, 9*, 466–486.

Ellison, L., & Munro, V. (2009). Reacting to rape: Exploring mock jurors' assessment of complainant credibility. *British Journal of Criminology, 49*, 202–219.

Fanflick, P.L. (2007). *Victim responses to sexual assault: Counterintuitive or simply adaptive* (Special Topic Series). Alexandria, VA: National District Attorney's Association

Frank, E., & Anderson, P. (1987). Psychiatric disorders in rape victims: Past history and current symptomatology. *Comprehensive Psychiatry, 28*, 77–82.

Frazier, P. (1990). Victim attributions and postrape trauma. *Journal of Personality and Social Psychology, 59,* 298–304.

Frazier, P., & Borgida, E. (1992). Rape trauma syndrome: A review of case law and psychological research. *Law and Human Behavior, 16,* 293–311.

Frieze, I.H., Hymer, S., & Greenberg, M.S. (1987). Describing the crime victim: psychological reactions to victimization. *Professional Psychology, 18,* 299–315.

Golding, J.M., Fryman, H.M., Marsil, D.F., & Yozwiak, J.A. (2003). Big girls don't cry: The effect of child witness demeanor on juror decisions in a child sexual abuse trial. *Child Abuse & Neglect, 27,* 1311–1321.

Hackett, L., Day, A., & Mohr, P. (2008). Expectancy violation and perceptions of rape victim credibility. *Legal and Criminological Psychology, 13,* 323–334.

Hammock, G.S., & Richardson, D.R. (1997). Perceptions of rape: The influence of closeness of relationship, intoxication and sex of participant. *Violence and Victims, 12,* 237–246.

Horney, J. & Spohn, C. (1996). The influence of blame and believability factors on the processing of simple versus aggravated rape cases. *Criminology, 34,* 135–162

Horvath, M.A., & Brown, J. (Eds.) (2009). *Rape: Challenging contemporary thinking.* Devon, United Kingdom: Willan Publishing.

Kahn, A.S., & Mathie, V.A. (2000). Understanding the unacknowledged rape victim. In C.B. Travis & J.W. White (Eds.), *Sexuality, society, and feminism* (pp. 377–403). Washington, DC: American Psychological Association.

Kahn, A.S., Mathie, V.A., & Torgler, C. (1994). Rape scripts and rape acknowledgment. *Psychology of Women Quarterly, 18,* 53–66. doi:10.1111/j.1471-6402.1994.tb00296.x

Kaufmann, G., Drevland, G.C.B., Wessel, E., Overskeid, G., & Magnussen, S. (2003). The importance of being earnest: Displayed emotions and witness credibility. *Applied Cognitive Psychology, 17,* 21–34.

Orvis, B.R., Cunningham, J.D., & Kelley, H.H. (1975). A closer examination of causal inference: The roles of consensus, distinctiveness, and consistency information. *Journal of Personality and Social Psychology, 32,* 605–616.

Konradi, A. (1999). I don't have to be afraid of you: Rape survivors' emotion management in court. *Symbolic Interaction, 22,* 45–77.

Krahé, B., Temkin, J., & Bieneck, S. (2007). Schema-driven information processing in judgments about rape. *Applied Cognitive Psychology, 21,* 601–619.

Krulewitz, J.E. (1982). Reactions to rape victims: Effects of rape circumstances, victims' emotional response, and sex of helper. *Journal of Consulting Psychology, 29,* 645–654.

Larcombe, W. (2002). The 'ideal' victim v successful rape complaints: Not what you might expect. *Feminist Legal Studies, 10,* 131–148.

Lonsway, K.A., & Fitzgerald, L.F. (1994). Rape myths: In review. *Psychology of Women Quarterly, 18,* 133–164.

Lonsway, K.A., & Fitzgerald, L.F. (1995). Attitudinal antecedents of rape myth acceptance: A theoretical and empirical reexamination. *Journal of Personality and Social Psychology, 68,* 704–711.

Matoesian, G.M. (1993). *Reproducing rape: Domination through talk in the courtroom.* Cambridge, UK: Polity Press.

Meyer, C., & Taylor, S. (1986). Adjustment to rape. *Journal of Personality and Social Psychology, 50,* 1226–1234.

Peterson, Z.D., & Muehlenhard, C.L. (2004). Was it rape? The function of women's rape myth acceptance and definitions of sex labeling their own experiences. *Sex Roles, 51,* 129–144.

Petrak, J., & Hedge, B. (2001). *The trauma of sexual assault: Treatment, prevention and practice.* New York: John Wiley & Sons, Inc.

Rodman, C.D. (1997). *Perceptions of stress associated with victim coping and dating outcome: Assessing the effects of respondent gender, sex-role and victimization status within an Air Force basic trainee population.* (Unpublished dissertation research). University of Arkansas.

Schuller, R.A., McKimmie, B.M., Masser, B.M., & Klippenstine, M.A. (2010). The impact of complainant emotional demeanor, gender, and victim stereotypes. *New Criminal Law Review, 13,* 759–780.

Schuller, R.A., & Hastings, P.A. (2002). Complainant sexual history evidence: Its impact on mock jurors decisions. *Psychology of Women Quarterly, 26,* 252–261.

Schuller, R.A., & Wall, A.M. (1998). The effects of defendant and complainant intoxication on mock jurors' judgements of sexual assault. *Psychology of Women Quarterly, 22*, 555–573.

Temkin, J., & Krahé, B. (2008). *Sexual and the justice gap: A question of attitude.* Portland, Oregon: Hart Publishing.

Vrij, A., & Fisher, F. (1996). The role of displays of emotions and ethnicity in judgments of rape victims. *International Review of Victimology, 4*, 255–265.

Wall, A.M., & Schuller, R.A. (2000). Sexual assault and defendant/victim intoxication: Jurors' perceptions of guilt. *Journal of Applied Social Psychology, 30*, 253–274.

Wessel, E., Drevland, G.C.B., & Eilertsen, D.E. (2006). Credibility of the emotional witness: A study of ratings by court judges. *Law and Human Behavior, 30*, 221–230.

Winkel, F.W., & Koppelaar, L. (1991). Rape victim's style of self-presentation and secondary victimization by the environment: An experiment. *Journal of Interpersonal Violence, 6*, 29–40.

Wortman, C.B. (1983). Coping with victimization: Conclusions and implications for future research. *Journal of Social Issues, 39*, 195–221.

Wyatt, G.E., Notgrass, C.M., & Newcomb, M. (1990). Internal and external mediators of women's rape experiences. *Psychology of Women Quarterly, 14*, 153–176.

Terminating parental rights: the relation of judicial experience and expectancy-related factors to risk perceptions in child protection cases

Alicia Summers[a], Sophia Gatowski[b] and Shirley Dobbin[b]

[a]National Council of Juvenile and Family Court Judges, Reno, Nevada, USA;
[b]Systems Change Solutions, Inc., White Rock, B.C., Canada

This study examined the impact of judicial experience and expectancy-related case factors on perceptions of risk in decisions to terminate parental rights. One hundred and thirty-three child abuse and neglect court judges read a simulated child protection case and decided whether to terminate parental rights. Three expectancy-related case factors (sibling presence, parent support, and information regarding the child's potential adoptability) were varied across eight experimental conditions. Data regarding judges' experience, emotion, cognitive style, and certain demographic variables were analyzed in relation to their perceptions of risk for the child returning home and the child remaining in foster care. Expectancy-related case factors predicted risk perception for experienced judges only. In contrast, emotion, cognitive style, and demographic variables predicted less experienced judges' decisions.

Introduction

Child protection[1] courts play a critical role in community responses to child abuse and neglect. Child protection court judges must make decisions about child safety, permanency and well-being within a legal framework that often requires psychological and social decision-making processes – they must balance the often-competing interests of the parents with the state and with the 'best interests' of the child. In addition, judges must depend primarily on the information provided to them by professionals to assist the court in interpreting the complex evidence to decide what the most appropriate outcomes are for children (Clark, 1995). This information may be difficult to obtain or of questionable reliability and there is a lack of specific guidelines to help judges determine what aspects of this information should be prioritized. Moreover, because of concerns about children lingering in foster care, judges must make child protection decisions within statutorily mandated timeframes that shorten the acceptable time for case processing and the achievement of case outcomes (e.g. Adoption and Safe Families Act, 1997).

Of all the judicial decisions in the child protection context, perhaps one of the most difficult is the termination of parental rights (TPR), which legally severs any relationship between parent and child (Ellis, Malm, & Bishop, 2009). A TPR ends all the rights and obligations that a parent has towards the child and is the 'family law equivalent of the death penalty in a criminal case' (In re Smith et al., 1991, p. 31). After a child has been placed in foster care and has substantiated allegations of abuse or neglect, the judge continuously must make decisions about a permanent plan for the child based on a standard of what is in the 'child's best interests'. Ultimately, that permanent plan may mean reunification or termination of parental rights. One of the primary factors influencing this decision is the perception of risk to the child, both the risk of returning the child home and the risk of the child remaining in foster care. It is largely unknown how judges actually make assessments of risk in termination of parental rights decisions, the factors they weigh and the information, beliefs, and experiences they draw upon. The current study seeks to fill this gap by examining case factors, experience, beliefs, demographic factors and expectancies that influence judicial perceptions of risk in a mock child abuse and neglect termination of parental rights case.

Judicial decision making in termination of parental rights cases

Civil child abuse and neglect cases present a complex case type with a great deal of judicial discretion, especially concerning variables such as the perception of risk in termination of parental rights cases. Risk in this context refers to the perceived risk to the safety, permanency and well-being of the child if the child is returned home to his or her biological parent, or the perceived risk to the safety, permanency and well-being of the child if he or she is to remain in another placement such as a foster home. Researchers have yet to focus on specific research related to judicial decision making in perceptions of risk. However, research on child protection workers and legal decision making may provide some insight. Case factors, experience, emotion, cognitive styles, and demographics for example, influence judicial decision making. Drawing upon past research, the current study examines how these factors might influence juvenile dependency court judges' perceptions of risk in simulated termination of parental rights decisions.

Case factors

Case level factors can significantly influence decisions in child abuse and neglect cases. Although research on judges is limited, some work points to case factors that may influence decision making. A review of relevant literature found that child age, parental functioning, availability of social support and the quality of the parent–child relationship influence child welfare workers' decisions to remove a child from the home (English, 1997). Qualitative research assessments of judicial decisions also indicate that judges consider (i.e. discuss) key case factors such as presence of a sibling, whether the home is a single parent home and the child's age and developmental status when making specific custody decisions (Wallace & Koerner, 2003). Although it was unclear from the study exactly how all of these factors influence the decisions, it is apparent that case level factors do play a key role in how judges make legal rulings. At a minimum, it appears that positive factors, such as parental support, might make judges more lenient toward parents, whereas factors such as substance abuse might lead judges to hold more negative views about parents. These factors may affect judges differently depending on their experience.

Experience

All judges are trained to understand and apply the law. Yet, child abuse and neglect cases present a unique legal opportunity to impact a case at multiple points and make decisions based on the law in the current context. As such, judges who have extensive experience or extensive training in making decisions in child abuse and neglect cases may make different decisions than newer or less experienced judges, simply because they have learned more about the complex nature of decision making with this population of cases.

Most researchers agree that experience plays a role in becoming an expert (Klein, 1997). Researchers believe that experts' decision-making process differs from that of non-experts (Phillips, Klein, & Sieck, 2004). The difference in decision making may be because experts have more procedural knowledge to draw upon when making their decisions (Drury-Hudson, 1999). Experts can use this knowledge and experiences to fill in missing gaps in order to better predict future experiences (Phillips et al., 2004). This may be because of their ability to discriminate between similar items, more accurately identifying the relevant information (Shanteau, Weiss, Thomas, & Pounds, 2003). Experts may then perceive risk differently because they are better at making predictions based on their experiences. In child abuse and neglect cases, experienced judges may be better able to discriminate which information is diagnostic (Shanteau, 1992) and better use that information in their decision making than less experienced judges.

Emotion

Emotion may also play a role in judicial decision making in child abuse and neglect cases. Child abuse cases can be very traumatic. Both social workers and police report responding very emotionally, both with anger and empathy when exposed to child abuse cases (Cheung & McNeil Boutte-Queen, 2000), and social workers report distress when responding to child abuse calls (Munro, 2005). Research in the area of jury decision making has already demonstrated that emotion can positively and negatively influence conviction rates. Anger toward the defendant enhances the likelihood of conviction (Bright & Goodman-Delahunty, 2006), while sympathy for the defendant decreases probability of conviction (Gastwirth & Sinclair, 2004). Emotion can enhance heuristic and inhibit systematic processing in legal cases (Feigenson & Park, 2006; Lieberman, 2002). Emotion may trigger a heuristic such as the attractiveness heuristic and make jurors more lenient toward an attractive defendant (Lieberman, 2002). Emotion may have a mood-congruent effect whereby the juror makes legal decisions based on positive or negative affect toward the defendant without paying attention to all relevant case factors (Feigenson & Park, 2006). Although this work has not been replicated, research on jurors and social workers indicates that emotion does play a role in processing child abuse and neglect case information. The negative response to the cases may result in harsher decisions towards parents.

Cognitive styles

Cognitive Experiential Self-Theory (CEST) is one of several dual processing theories (Chaiken & Trope, 1999; Epstein, 1990, 1994). It posits that individuals can process information through two distinct, yet interrelated systems: a rational and an experiential system. The rational system constitutes effortful, logical, and systematic processing, while the experiential system constitutes automatic, heuristic, emotional processing. Individuals can engage in either rational or experiential processing, depending on how they are cued to think and their motivation (Kirkpatrick & Epstein, 1992). CEST assumes that systematic and automatic processing are interrelated systems and that individuals can utilize one or both simultaneously or easily switch between the two (Kirkpatrick & Epstein, 1992). This means that individuals can go from effortful to effortless processing and vice versa.

The type of processing may affect how individuals perceive information. While rational processing is more process oriented, experiential processing is more outcome focused and action-oriented. This may mean that individuals who are processing experientially may look at the 'big picture', but overlook important details that could influence the decision making process (Kirkpatrick & Epstein, 1992). Although one can switch between processing styles, the current processing style may bias the other. For example, Chaiken's work, among others, suggests that experiential processing may cause individuals to overlook information on which a rational processor might focus (Chaiken & Maheswaran, 1994).

Research has already demonstrated that CEST has applicability to the field of jury decision making. The type of processing an individual is using can influence verdict and sentencing decisions (Lieberman, 2002). However, the exact role of CEST in judicial decision making is unclear, particularly in cases concerning obscure concepts such as those related to risk. Further, the interaction of judicial experience and cognitive processing is unknown. The possibility that experience and cognitive processing may significantly influence judicial decision making in child abuse and neglect cases warrants further investigation.

Demographics

Demographic characteristics, such as gender and parental status may also influence child abuse and neglect case decisions. Prior research has shown that females and parents of either gender have a stronger emotional reaction to child abuse and neglect cases than do males and individuals without children (Stone & Taylor, 1981). Further, research has shown that females and parents are often more conviction prone (Golding, Bradshaw, Dunlap, & Hodell, 2007). Age may also be a factor, with some research indicating that younger adults view risk differently than older adults (Steinberg, 2008). These demographic differences may play a role in perception of risk in legal decision making.

Expectancy

Research clearly indicates there are case factors that predict social worker and judicial decisions. What is not clear is how these factors influence decisions. Perhaps the best explanation for why some of these factors may be particularly relevant is that they are inconsistent with what the judge is expecting. In research on TPR decisions, nearly all (96%) of cases that came before a judge (or jury) for a TPR trial ended with termination of parental rights (Children's Action Alliance, 2005). It is logical to assume, then, that when a case comes before a judge for a TPR hearing that the expectation is that the case will end in termination. Part of this expectancy is most likely due to the legal criteria associated with TPR decisions. According to the Adoption and Safe Families Act (ASFA), the agency is required to file a termination of parental rights petition if the child has been in foster care for at least 15 of the last 22 months (US PL 105–89). The child's length of placement in foster care is completely objective and verifiable by facts, such as recorded placement history. Therefore, it can be assumed that when a TPR case comes before the court, this legal criterion has definitely been met.

There are, however, exceptions to this rule. Many states have additional criteria including that terminating parent rights must also be in the child's best interest. The best interest criterion is subjective. The party filing for termination may believe that termination is in the child's best interest for a variety of reasons, but their decision making may be quite different from the judges. This is supported by research that has demonstrated that judges and social workers rely on different information when making placement decisions in child welfare cases (Britner & Mossler, 2002). There may be facts in the case that will lead judges to determine that termination is not in the child's best interest. Discussions with expert judges who serve as judicial trainers indicated that there are factors that may lead a judge not to terminate parental rights. Specifically, presence of a sibling, presence of a support system, and adoptability of the child were identified as potential factors linked with a decision not to terminate parental rights. Prior research focused on caseworkers and judges confirms that siblings, support, and adoptability all play a role in decision making (Ellis et al., 2009; English, 1997; Wallace & Koerner, 2003). If a judge gets a TPR case, and most of the legal criteria is objective, it seems there would be an expectancy that termination will occur; particularly if as many as 96% of termination filings result in termination (Children's Action Alliance, 2005). Yet, if the above-mentioned factors are present, this may violate the judges' expectations and cause them to reconsider terminating parent rights. This is because violations of expectations affect cognitive processing.

Research on expectancies has demonstrated that information that violates expectations is remembered just as well, if not better, than information that is consistent with expectations (Stangor & McMillan, 1992). Judges may be more likely to recall the expectancy inconsistent case factors, and therefore rely on them more heavily in their decision making. This may be because expectancy inconsistent information increases rational processing (Maheswaran & Chaiken, 1991). When subjects were presented with messages that were not congruent with expectancies, they tended to process rationally (Maheswaran & Chaiken, 1991). If information is inconsistent with expectancies, judges may engage in rational processing, which may ensure better memory for and use of the information in decision making. Using expectancy inconsistent case factors can help researchers to ascertain whether these factors predict risk decisions.

Overview and hypotheses

Related literature indicates that there might be multiple factors that can influence assessment of risk in termination of parental rights decisions. Expectancy inconsistent case factors, experience, emotion, cognitive styles and demographics may all play a role in the decision making process. Yet, how these factors influence risk perception is unknown. In particular, the effects of case factors and of judicial experience require more attention. It may be that expectancy inconsistent case factors will cause judges to engage in more rational processing, causing them to reconsider the decision to terminate and likewise decreasing their perception of risk.

Case factors are only one part of the equation. The other consideration is the role of experience. Child abuse cases are complex and require multiple decisions across the life of the case. Experts in the field recommend that judges that oversee these case types have longer rotations in order to gain experience with and better understand child abuse cases (see Edwards, 2005). Experienced judges may rely on different decision-making factors than less experienced judges, which may influence outcome decisions. Therefore, any examination of child abuse cases must account for experience of the judge. The current study seeks to assess the role of experience and expectancy inconsistent case factors, while also examining other predictive factors, such as emotion, cognitive styles and demographics and their relationship to perceptions of risk in termination of parent rights decisions.

> *Hypothesis 1:* Decisions to terminate will be associated with higher perceived risk of returning the child home and lower perceived risk of leaving the child in foster care.
>
> *Hypothesis 2:* Expectancy-related case factors will predict perceptions of risk for high experienced judges; whereas emotion, cognitive style, and certain demographic characteristics will predict perceptions of risk for less experienced judges.
>
> Hypothesis 3: Cognitive styles will be significant predictors for low experience judges but not for high experience judges. Less experienced judges who tend to process rationally will perceive less risk to the child of returning home and more risk of leaving the child in foster care. Less experienced judges who process more experientially will perceive more risk to the child of returning home and less risk of the child remaining in foster care.

Method

Participants

One hundred and thirty-three judges, recruited from the National Council of Juvenile and Family Court Judges' (National Council) judicial membership list, participated in the study. The National Council is the oldest judicial membership organization in the United States, founded in 1937 to provide training to the nation's juvenile and family court judges. The entire judicial membership ($N = 1585$) was sent an email, asking them to participate in a study on judicial decisions. The recruitment email did have a caveat that requested only judges who at some point in their career had overseen child abuse and neglect cases. The first question on the survey was a screening tool that ended participation if the participant responded 'no' they had never overseen child abuse cases. The participation rate was approximately 10% of the membership; however, dependency judges are estimated to make up one-third of the membership, which indicates approximately 30% of the judges applicable to participate, did so. Judges were male (65%), Caucasian (95%), and reported that they were parents themselves (90%). On average, participants were 54 years old. All of the judges who participated had overseen child protection cases (dependency or child abuse and neglect cases) at some point in their judicial career and 89% currently had a child protection caseload. On average, judges had spent 9 years overseeing child protection cases (SD = 6.64) and had participated in approximately 106 hours of specific training related to this case type (SD = 134.89).

Materials

Case scenario

A case scenario of a child protection case at the termination of parental rights trial phase was given to the respondent judges. The case scenario, which was constructed from actual child abuse and neglect case files, involved a mother with substance abuse issues who had substantiated allegations of abuse and neglect for taking her 8-year-old child into a known residence with drug dealers. The language in the case scenario was consistent with actual termination cases in which substance abuse was a contributing factor. We examined real case files used in training exercises at the National Council during the instrument modification process in order to make the case scenario as realistic as possible. Interviews with expert judges in termination of parental rights trials were conducted to determine what case factors might have violated expectancies, preventing the termination of parental rights. The judges identified presence of a sibling, presence of support, and the adoptability of the child as key factors (these key factors were also identified in a study by Ellis *et al.* (2009) in which judges from around the country were interviewed about the termination of parental rights). Two expert judges also vetted the case scenario and provided feedback on its authenticity and appropriateness for the current project. The final case scenario was four single-spaced pages with an additional one-page case petition. The case scenario outlined relevant case facts, included a copy of the child abuse and neglect petition, a summary of all of the legal findings throughout the case and testimony from all parties. The case scenario indicated that the allegations of child abuse and neglect were substantiated at a prior hearing and that the child had been in foster care for the last 17 months. The mother had only recently begun to comply with the case plan. The facts varied on inclusion of three case level expectancy inconsistent relevant factors: (1) presence of siblings, (2) parental involvement in a Narcotics Anonymous (NA) support group, and (3) statistical information regarding the child's potential adoptability.

For the sibling condition, participants read that the mother had given birth to another child during the course of the case. Because the mother was in compliance at the time the new child was born, this child was not removed from her care. The NA support condition indicated that the mother had recently begun attending NA meetings and had established a support system. The third factor was a statistic on the adoptability of the child, indicating that at the child's current age, he is unlikely to be adopted (adoptability statistics are commonly presented in these cases). All three of these facts were hypothesized to be inconsistent with expectancies in decisions to terminate parental rights. Each case scenario had some combination of these facts. This resulted in one of eight possible scenarios for the judge-participants.

Dependent measures

Outcome decision

After reading the case scenario, judges rendered decisions regarding the termination of parental rights by choosing one of two options: 'terminate' or 'do not terminate'.

Perception of risk

Following the outcome decision, judges indicated their perceptions of risk to the child on two risk factors using an eight-point scale ranging from 0 (*not at all*) to 7 (*high risk*). The first perception of risk was the risk of returning the child to the home immediately. The second factor was the risk to the child if the child remained in foster care.

Experience

Judges were asked to indicate their level of experience (in years) overseeing child abuse and neglect cases. They were also asked to indicate a number of hours of training they had received in the area of child abuse and neglect.

Emotion

Respondent judges were asked to indicate their current levels of negative emotion. Using a slightly condensed, 10-item version of the Juror Negative Affect Scale (JUNAS; Bright & Goodman-Delahunty, 2006), participants rated the extent to which they had felt specific emotions *in response to the case scenario.* These negative emotions included items related to anger, fear or anxiety, sadness and disgust. Responses were on a five-point scale ranging from *not at all* to *extremely.*

Cognitive style

Judges also completed a measure of cognitive style. The Rational–Experiential Inventory (REI) measures self-reported personality traits related to preference for rational and experiential processing (Epstein, Pacini, Denes-Raj, & Heier, 1996). Participants identified how true a series of statements was for them ranging from 1 (*completely false*) to 5 (*completely true*). This scale includes two subscales – a short version of the Need for Cognition (i.e. Rational) scale and a constructed Faith in Intuition (i.e. Experiential) scale. The faith in intuition subscale measures tendency toward processing experientially (e.g. 'I believe in trusting my hunches'), while the need for cognition subscale measures the tendency toward rational processing (e.g. 'I prefer complex to simple problems').

Expectation violation check

To determine if the case factors actually violated an expectation of termination, judges were also asked to complete a rational processing measure. As indicated above, expectancy inconsistent information is supposed to encourage rational processing. If these factors actually violated the judge's expectations, the judges in these conditions should process more rationally than judges in the condition without the factors. The measure included two CEST vignettes (Epstein, Lipson, Holstein, & Huh, 1992). The CEST vignettes included short scenarios about two characters that have the same outcome based on differing decisions. For example, in one scenario Mr Paul decides to take stocks from company A and then discovers he would have made substantial money had he stayed with company A. Mr George almost decides to switch to company A but decides against it and also learns he would have made money had he switched. Participants evaluated which character was more foolish in their decision. The rational response is that both are equally foolish, while experiential processors are more likely to indicate that one character is more foolish than the other is.

Demographics

Finally, judges were asked for basic demographic information, including age, gender, and parental status.

Procedure

Once judges agreed to participate in the study, they were given a web site link that randomly sent them to one of eight research conditions. Participants read the case scenario and responded to the subsequent questions on outcome, risk, experience, emotion, cognitive style, and demographics.

Coding of variables

Before analysis, a number of the variables of interest to the study required computations. First, to assess negative emotion, an average negative emotion score was calculated from all 10 negative emotions listed in the modified JUNAS scale. The scale showed good internal consistency with a Cronbach alpha coefficient of 0.88. Next, the REI experiential and rational subscale computations were generated. Items on the REI that were rational were averaged, as were items that were experiential, resulting in two variables – the REI_Experiential and the REI_Rational. Higher numbers on these scales indicated higher degrees of the trait (i.e. high REI_Rational indicated personality traits that enjoy rational processing). Both the REI_Rational and the REI_Experiential scales demonstrated adequate reliability ($\alpha = 0.87, 0.68$, respectively). For the CEST measures, if the judge responded with the correct answer (i.e. characters were equal in CEST measures), they were scored as rational, whereas incorrect responses were scored as irrational. Responses from the two were averaged for a rational processing score ranging from 0 *experiential* to 1 *rational*.

Results

The purpose of the analyses was to determine which factors affect juvenile dependency court judges' perceptions of risk in termination of parental rights cases. The underlying assumption for this assessment (Hypothesis 1) was that risk was related to decisions to terminate parental rights. Preliminary analyses indicated that perceptions of risk were the strongest factors related to the decision to terminate parental rights. A binary logistic regression ascertained the relationship between risk perception and the decision to terminate parental rights. The overall model was significant ($\chi^2(3) = 75.58$, $p < 0.001$; $f^2 = 0.74$). Perception of risk of returning the child home now ($b = -0.64$, Wald $= 6.16$, $p < 0.05$, OR $= 0.52$) and risk of leaving the child in foster care ($b = 0.497$, Wald $= 7.19$, $p < 0.01$, OR $= 1.64$) were both significantly related to termination decisions. Judges who were more likely to terminate parental rights saw higher risks of returning the child home. Termination decisions were negatively related to the perceived risk of leaving the child in foster care such that judges who were less likely to terminate parental rights perceived a higher risk of leaving the child in foster care than those who terminated parental rights. This supported Hypothesis 1.

Prior to the analyses, we examined the experience and training of judges in order to separate them into high and low experience judges. Years of experience was significantly correlated with hours of trainings ($r = 0.39$, $p < 0.01$), therefore, we decided to simplify the analysis by using only experience. The median number of years experience was eight. Using a median split, we divided judges into low experience and high experience (experienced) judges. We then compared high experience to low experience judges to determine if they varied significantly on any of the predictor variables. The two subsets were equitable on all factors, except age. High experience judges were significantly older ($M = 56$, SD $= 6.6$) than low experience judges ($M = 52$, SD $= 7.9$), although the difference appears marginal.

Expectancy violation check

The three case variables were meant to violate the expectations of the judges. Based on prior research, expectancy inconsistent information should be easily recalled (Stangor & McMillan, 1992) and should engage rational processing (Maheswaran & Chaiken, 1991). Two measures assessed the impact of the expectancy inconsistent variables. First, we asked judges (after making their outcome decision), which factors they relied upon most heavily in making their decision. We coded responses when they included the expectancy inconsistent factors. For low experience judges, both sibling ($b = 1.55$ Wald $= 4.42$, $p < 0.05$) and adoptable ($b = 1.39$, Wald $= 3.58$, $p = 0.06$) factors predicted recalling these facts as important. For high experience judges, only the sibling factor was significant in predicting recall of the variable ($b = 1.49$, Wald $= 6.19$, $p < 0.01$). We also examined the factors in predicting rational processing using the CEST measure. In this analysis, none of the expectancy inconsistent information predicted rational processing for low experience judges. However, for experienced judges, both the sibling condition ($\beta = 0.19$, $p < 0.05$) and the adoptable condition ($\beta = 0.20$, $p < 0.05$) predicted rational processing. Being in these conditions increased the likelihood of rational processing for experienced judges. The results supported the notion that at least two of the case factors violated expectations. We included all three variables in the analyses in order to look at differences that might emerge and to control for case type.

In order to ascertain the differences in the decision making process of judges (Hypothesis 2), a series of linear regression models were used to assess the impact of case factors, emotion, cognitive style, and demographics on perceptions of risk. We ran the series of models separately for low experience and high experience judges.

Risk of returning the child home right now

The first assessment of risk examined perception of risk to the child if he was returned home to his parent right now. On average, judges indicated moderate to high perception of risk of returning home right now ($M = 4.56$, SD $= 1.73$). There were no significant differences in low and high experience judges' perceptions of risk of returning the child home right now. In order to examine Hypothesis 2, we examined predictive factors for both low and high experience judges.

Low experience judges

The first model determined if the expectancy inconsistent case factors predicted risk. For low experience judges, none of the case factors significantly predicted perception of risk of returning the child home right now. The second model examined the effect of negative emotion on perception of risk. Negative emotion significantly predicted risk ($R^2 = 0.15$, $F(1,60) = 3.48$, $p < 0.05$; $f^2 = 0.17$). Increases in negative emotion predicted increases in perception of risk for returning the child home ($\beta = 0.32$, $p < 0.01$), supporting Hypothesis 2. The third model examined cognitive styles, which did not significantly predict risk, failing to support Hypothesis 3. The final model examined demographic factors and their relationship to risk. The overall model was not significant. None of the demographics significantly predicted risk, although age approached significance ($\beta = 0.25$, $p = 0.07$).

High experience judges

The same series of linear regressions was conducted for the high experience judges. For experienced judges, the case factors were the best predictors of risk ($R^2 = 0.42$, $F(3,59) = 13.70$, $p < 0.001$; $f^2 = 0.72$). Both the sibling condition ($\beta = -0.53$, $p < 0.001$) and the NA support condition ($\beta = -0.27$, $p < 0.01$) predicted perception of risk. Judges in these conditions perceived less risk to the child of returning home, supporting Hypothesis 2. None of the other factors were significant predictors, even when controlling for the significant case factors. The results of the models are reported in Table 1.

Risk of leaving the child in foster care

The second perception of risk variable asked judges to indicate their assessment of the risk to the child if he or she was to stay in foster care. On average, judges felt that there was a moderate to high level of risk to the child of remaining in foster care ($M = 4.47$, SD $= 1.66$). There were no differences in low experience judges and high experience judges in perception of risk of the child remaining in foster care.

Table 1. Predictors of perceived risk of returning the child home right now.

	Low experience judges		High experience judges	
	β	p	β	p
Expectancy inconsistent case factors				
Sibling Present	−0.18	0.19	−0.53	0.00*
NA Support Group	−0.04	0.74	−0.27	0.01*
Adoptable Statistic	−0.10	0.47	−0.11	0.30
Emotion				
Negative Emotion	0.34	0.01*	0.09	0.38
Cognitive styles				
REI_Rational	−0.09	0.50	−0.07	0.52
REI_Experiential	0.16	0.87	−0.05	0.65
Demographics				
Female	0.16	0.24	0.10	0.37
Age	−0.20	0.13	−0.05	0.65
Parent	0.25	0.07	−0.02	0.85

*$p < 0.05$.

Low experience judges

The initial model examined the expectancy inconsistent case level factors and was not quite significant ($R^2 = 0.11$, $F(3,61) = 2.31$, $p = 0.08$; $f^2 = 0.12$). However, one of the case level factors was significant. Judges in the adoptability condition ($\beta = 0.29$, $p < 0.05$) perceived higher risks for children in foster care. Negative emotion was not a significant predictor. The model for cognitive style was significant ($R^2 = 0.11$, $F(2,59) = 3.63$, $p < 0.05$; $f^2 = 0.13$). Higher levels of REI_Rational processing predicted higher perception of risk ($\beta = 0.25$, $p < 0.05$), while lower level of REI_Experiential processing predicted higher perception of risk to child of remaining in foster care ($\beta = 0.25$, $p < 0.05$). This partially supports Hypothesis 3. The fourth model examined demographic predictors of perception of risk. This model was also significant ($R^2 = 0.32$, $F(3,60) = 6.37$, $p < 0.001$; $f^2 = 0.32$). Age significantly predicted perception of risk to the child in foster care ($\beta = 0.43$, $p < 0.001$), with older adults perceiving more risk. This partially supports Hypothesis 2.

High experience judges

We ran the same series of linear regression models for the experienced judges. Unlike the low experience judges, none of the models was significant or even approached statistical significance, failing to support Hypothesis 2. Results of the models are reported in Table 2.

Discussion

The current study sought to fill a gap in the literature base by examining experience and expectancies in perceptions of risk in termination of parent rights trials. The

Table 2. Predictors of perceived risk of leaving the child in foster care.

	Low experience judges		High experience judges	
	β	p	β	p
Expectancy inconsistent case factors				
Sibling Present	0.84	0.40	0.00	0.98
NA Support Group	0.37	0.72	−0.07	0.59
Adoptable Statistic	0.29	0.02*	−0.21	0.84
Emotion				
Negative Emotion	−0.16	0.21	0.04	0.55
Cognitive styles				
REI_Rational	0.25	0.05*	−0.14	0.31
REI_Experiential	−0.25	0.05*	−0.02	0.86
Demographics				
Female	0.19	0.12	0.24	0.08
Age	−0.43	0.01*	0.21	0.12
Parent	−0.18	0.15	−0.04	0.78

*$p < 0.05$.

initial analysis supported Hypothesis 1, indicating that risk perception is strongly related to the decision to terminate parental rights. Following the initial assessment, we wanted to determine how experience and expectancies affected risk assessments. In Hypothesis 2, we predicted that experienced judges would rely on different decision-making factors than low experience judges. This hypothesis was supported. In the first series of assessments examining risk of returning the child home right now, we discovered that emotion was a significant predictor for low experience judges but not high experience judges. This may be attributed to the fact that low experience judges are more emotionally responsive to the case compared high experience judges. The novelty of the traumatic cases may cause negative emotions, which may influence their decision making. Although emotion seems to be a normal reaction to a child abuse case, this may be detrimental to making an informed decision. Emotion can trigger heuristic processing, causing a lack of attention to important details. In this case, the judges appeared to be overlooking the case factors when they made a decision regarding perceived risk. These factors were not significant predictors of risk, indicating little attention paid to them. They did remember the factors (as evidenced by the expectancy violation check questions), yet they did not allow these factors to influence their decisions. In the real world, this lack of attention to relevant information could be very detrimental, particularly if judges overlook factors that could deter termination and help to reunite a child with his family. This is further evidenced by the results related to high experience judges.

For high experience judges, the expectancy inconsistent case factors were the best predictors. This means that the high experience judges were more likely to pay attention to the relevant case facts, designed to discourage termination. This, combined with the fact that the expectancy inconsistent factors made high experience judges more likely to engage in rational processing indicates that experience might play a big role in how judges make decisions. High experience judges may be more aware of which factors are inconsistent with expectations and might respond to them accordingly. Low experience judges, however, may not have clear expectations, and may rely on other sources of information to inform their decision, such as the negative emotions they experience.

The comparisons for risk of leaving the child in foster care demonstrated quite different results. The case factors were meant to discourage termination and indicate less risk of returning home. Yet, there were no factors directed toward foster care placement. Therefore, judges had to rely on other information to make this assessment. None of the factors was predictive for high experience judges, while cognitive processing, age, and the adoptability factor all predicted low experience judges perceptions of risk. Those who preferred rational processing saw more risk, while experiential processors saw less risk. Older adults saw more risk, as did those in the adoptability condition. These findings indicate that perhaps, when there is no clearly relevant case or legal factor to rely upon, low experience judges are more likely to fall back on personal predispositions when making decisions. High experience judges, on the other hand, show no such trend. Perhaps high experience judges have greater knowledge of risks in foster care because of their greater experience, and thus need not rely on personal beliefs when making their decisions.

The differences between predictive factors for perception of risk of returning the child home compared to perception of risk of leaving the child in foster care were quite interesting. One might assume that the risk of returning the child home and the risk of leaving the child in foster care are two sides of the same coin. In some ways they are. If the child is not returned home, it is likely that he will remain in foster care. Yet, this is an oversimplification of the issue. If the risk of returning home is high, then it might be in the child's best interest to terminate parental rights. Terminating parental rights also frees the child for adoption, which will ultimately remove him from foster care as well. The distinction between the two perceptions of risk may be further explained by the fact that the judicial decisions in child abuse cases focus primarily on how the parent is doing. Judges rely heavily on information regarding parental compliance and progress toward meeting their case plan when they make their decisions to terminate parental rights (Ellis et al., 2009). In fact, throughout the case, judges focus primarily on the parent to make decisions regarding placement, visitation and eventually outcome. The risk in foster care, however, is not something that requires a legal decision.

Another thought on the difference between the two perceptions of risk is that this supports the notion that less experienced judges rely on different case factors than experienced judges. For example, the adoptability of the child was a significant predictor of perceived risk in foster care for low experience judges only. This may be because high experience judges are already familiar with the statistics on adoptability or may be aware due to their own experiences that older youth are less likely to be adopted. The adoptability statistic may have violated low experience judges' expectations about the risks in foster care. This could also explain why the rational processors saw more risk and the experiential processors saw less risk. The expectation violation caused the rational processors to think more about the issue, increasing their perception of risk.

These results clearly signify that experience and expectancies are important factors in judicial decision making. Expectancy inconsistent information was a strong predictor of high experience judges' decisions in risk assessment, which affects outcome decisions such as termination of parental rights. High experience judges accurately rely on information that is counter to their expectations and correctly use it in decision making. Low experience judges, however, do not use this information. Although there was no statistical difference in risk perception overall, the process by which judges reached this information appears to be very different. This has serious implications for juvenile court judges. Low experience judges may not be adequately equipped to recognize important case factors, which may ultimately lead to incorrect decisions. This lends support to suggestions for increased judicial rotation in order to for judges to understand child abuse cases better (Edwards, 2005). With increased judicial rotations, judges would get more experience on the bench, better learning about child abuse and neglect cases. With more experience, they will be able to identify the key factors that should be part of their decision-making process. Then, when case factors are presented that are contrary to certain decisions (e.g. termination), the judge will be better suited to make an informed decision.

Limitations

The current study has some limitations to note. A common complaint with this type of research is that it is not conducted in a naturalistic setting, which may make it less applicable to the real world (Ebbesen & Konečni, 1982). Real termination trials can be lengthy and will include more information than can be given in a case scenario; however, the case scenario was designed from real world materials and vetted with high experience judges for authenticity, with those high experience judges indicating that the information provided was typical of the information available at a termination trial. The current study attempted to make the case scenario as realistic as possible.

A second limitation to note was that the case scenario and case facts might have missed important factors that judges consider in their decision making. As noted by prior research, the parent–child relationship is an important factor in decision making (English, 1997; Wallace & Koerner, 2003). Judges who participated in this study also commented on the need for more information on the parent–child relationship or parent–child bond. It is apparent that this is an important decision-making factor and should have been included in the case scenario.

Another consideration is that there might have been order effects preventing more explicit analysis. Judges were asked to make a termination decision first, and then asked to predict risk, followed by other case questions. From this order, it is impossible to determine if risk perceptions predicted termination decisions. We can only determine that the two variables are related. The research study would be have enhanced if order effects had been considered and controlled for.

A final limitation is that the CEST measure was administered following judge's exposure to the simulated case scenario. Because the judges were not given the CEST measure before and after the case scenario, it is impossible to determine if the case factors elicited rational processing or if the judges were already processing rationally.

Future research

The current study provides a foundation from which additional research can begin. There is still much to do in the realm of juvenile dependency court judicial decision-making generally, and in the perceptions of risk in the termination of parental rights specifically. Future studies should focus more on specific definitions of risk and its influence on the decision-making process. For example, defining risk in terms of the child's physical safety versus the child's emotional well-being may yield considerable differences in how risk is viewed. By delineating the multiple concepts that risk entails, it is then possible to ascertain how risk is defined and how each varying level of risk may influence key court decisions.

Future studies should also consider other case factors, such as the parent–child relationship. This factor has already been identified as a significant factor in decision making (Ellis et al., 2009). By examining parent–child relationships in relation to risk perception, it will be possible to determine if the parent–child relationship affects perceptions of risk and subsequent case outcomes.

Another direction for future research is to do more work in the field. Working directly with judges, conducting focus groups and on-the-bench assessments of the decisions made in specific hearings, might lead to better insight into how judges view risk and how they use it in their decision-making process. Ideally, having judges evaluate specific risks in cases and following those cases to final case outcome could result in groundbreaking work related to judicial decision making and risk perception. This type of assessment could easily be used to better educate judges on perceptions of risk, how that can influence decisions and case outcomes, and help to formulate specific guidelines or recommendations to help judges make better informed decisions in the termination of parental rights. Further, exploring specific trainings and years of experience, can help determine how much experience is enough to recognize important case factors. By examining real world cases, researchers can determine how 'accurate' judicial decisions are, and help judges to improve these decisions in the future.

From a broader perspective, it may also be interesting to examine further the interaction of experience and expectancies. In this context, expectancy inconsistent information seemed to illicit rational processing and recall for high experience judges and affected their decision making when relevant. However, the effect was not the same for low experience judges. Future research may be able to determine if this is a context-specific effect or if experience is important in all cognitive processes related to expectancies.

Acknowledgements

The present research was supported by the University of Nevada, Reno Interdisciplinary Social Psychology program, the National Council of Juvenile and Family Court Judges and the American Psychology-Law Society.

Note

1. The term 'child protection courts' are used in this article to refer to courts hearing child abuse and neglect cases. These courts may be called child protection courts, or juvenile dependency courts, or child welfare courts.

References

Adoption and Safe Families Act (1997). US PL 105–89.
Bright, D.A., & Goodman-Delahunty, J. (2006). Gruesome evidence and emotion: Anger, blame, and jury decision-making. *Law and Human Behavior, 30*, 183–202.

Britner, P.A., & Mossler, D.G. (2002). Professional's decision-making about out-of-home placements following instances of child abuse. *Child Abuse and Neglect, 26,* 317–332.

Chaiken, S. & Maheswaran, D. (1994). Heuristic processing can bias systematic processing: Effects of source credibility, argument ambiguity, and task importance on attitude judgment. *Journal of Personality and Social Psychology, 66,* 460–473.

Chaiken, S., & Trope, Y. (1999). *Dual process theories in social psychology.* New York, NY: Guilford Press.

Cheung, M., & McNeil Boutte-Queen, N. (2000). Emotional responses to child sexual abuse: A comparison between police and social workers in Hong Kong. *Child Abuse and Neglect, 24,* 1613–1621. Retrieved from http://0-www.sciencedirect.com.innopac.library.unr.edu/science/journal/01452134

Children's Action Alliance. (May 2005). *Termination of parental rights by a jury trial in Arizona: A first year look.* Arizona Juvenile Courts.

Clark, R. (1995). Child protection and social work. In P.A. Swain (Ed.), *In the shadow of the law: The legal context of social work practice* (pp. 131–142). Sydney: Federation Press.

Drury-Hudson, J. (1999). Decision-making in child protection: The use of theoretical, empirical, and procedural knowledge by novices and experts and implications for fieldwork placement. *British Journal of Social Work, 29,* 147–169. Retrieved from http://bjsw.oxfordjournals.org

Ebbesen, E. B., & Konečni, V. J. (1982). Social psychology and the law: A decision making approach to the criminal justice system. In V. Konečni & E. Ebbesen (Eds.), *The Criminal Justice System: A Social-Psychological Analysis* (pp. 3–24). San Francisco, CA: W.H. Freeman and Company.

Edwards, L.P. (2005). The role of the Juvenile Court Judge Revisited. *Juvenile and Family Court Journal, 56,* 33–51.

Ellis, R., Malm, K., & Bishop, E.A. (2009). The timing of the termination of parental rights: A balancing act for children's best interests. *Child Trends Research Brief,* #2009-40.

English, D.J. (1997). Current knowledge about CPS decision-making. In T. D. Morton & W. Holder (Eds.), *Decision-making in children's protective services: Advancing the state of the art* (pp. 56–74). Atlanta, GA: Child Welfare Institute.

Epstein, S. (1990). Cognitive–experiential self-theory. In L. Pervin (Ed.), *Handbook of personality: Theory and research* (pp. 165–192). New York, NY: Guilford Press.

Epstein, S. (1994). Integration of the cognitive and the psychodynamic unconscious. *American Psychologist, 49,* 709–724.

Epstein, S., Pacini, R., Denes-Raj, V., & Heier, H. (1996). Individual differences in intuitive–experiential and analytical–rational thinking styles. *Journal of Personality and Social Psychology, 71*(2), 390–405.

Feigenson, N., & Park, J. (2006). Emotions and attributions of legal responsibility and blame: A research review. *Law and Human Behavior, 30,* 143–161.

Gastwirth, J.L., & Sinclair, M.D. (2004). A re-examination of the 1966 Kalven–Zeisel study of judge–jury agreements and disagreements and their causes. *Law, Probability, and Risk, 3,* 169–191.

Golding, J.M., Bradshaw, G.S., Dunlap, E.E., & Hodell, E.C. (2007). The impact of mock jury gender composition on deliberations and conviction rates in a child sexual assault trial. *Child Maltreatment, 12,* 182–190.

In re Smith et al., No. 90-OT-038, 77 Ohio App. 3d 1, 1991 Ohio App. LEXIS 4120 (E.D. Ohio, 30 August 1991).

Kirkpatrick, L.A., & Epstein, S. (1992). Cognitive–experiential self-theory and subjective probably: Further evidence for two conceptual frameworks. *Journal of Personality and Social Psychology, 63,* 534–544.

Klein, G. (1997). Developing expertise in decision-making. *Thinking and Reasoning, 3,* 337–352.

Lieberman, J.D. (2002). Head over heart or heart over the head? Cognitive experiential self-theory and extralegal heuristics in juror decision-making. *Journal of Applied Social Psychology, 32,* 2526–2553.

Maheswaran, D., & Chaiken, S. (1991). Promoting systemic processing in low-motivation settings: Effect of incongruent information on processing and judgment. *Journal of Personality and Social Psychology, 61*, 13–25.

Munro, E. (2005). Improving practice: Child protection as a systems problem. *Children and Youth Services Review, 27*, 375–391.

Phillips, J.K., Klein, G., & Sieck, W.R. (2004). Expertise in judgment and decision making: A case for training intuitive decision skills. In D. Koehler & N. Harvey (Eds.) *Blackwell Handbook of Judgment and Decision Making* (pp. 297–315). Malden, MA: Blackwell Publishing.

Shanteau, J. (1992). How much information does an expert use? Is it relevant? *Acta Psychologia, 81*, 75–86. Retrieved from http://www.elsevier.com/locate/actpsy

Shanteau, J., Weiss, D.J., Thomas, R.P., & Pounds, J. (2003). How can you tell if someone is an expert? Performance based assessment of expertise. In S. Schneider & J. Shanteau (Eds.), *Emerging perspectives on judgment and decision research* (pp. 620–639). New York, NY: Cambridge University Press.

Steinberg L. (2008). A social neuroscience perspective on adolescent risk-taking. *Developmental Review, 28*, 78–106.

Stone, L.E., & Taylor, B.K. (1981). Physiological responses to child abuse stimuli as criteria for selection of hotline counselors. *Journal of General Psychology, 104*, 103–110. Retrieved from http://www.tandf.co.uk/journals/titles/00221309.asp

Stangor, C., & McMillan, D. (1992). Memory for expectancy-congruent and expectancy-incongruent information: A review of the social and social developmental literatures. *Psychological Bulletin, 111*, 42–61.

Wallace, S.R., & Koerner, S.S. (2003). Influence of child and family factors on judicial decisions in contested custody cases. *Family Relations, 52*, 180–188. Retrieved from http://0-www.jstor.org.innopac.library.unr.edu/stable/3700221

Attorney and lay beliefs about factors affecting jurors' perceptions of juvenile offender culpability

Catherine R. Camilletti and Matthew H. Scullin

Department of Psychology, University of Texas at El Paso, El Paso USA

We surveyed attorneys and college students to learn what factors they believe influence jurors' perceptions of juvenile offender culpability and then varied two of these factors in a simulated case to determine their actual effects on mock jurors' decisions. In Study 1, attorneys ($N = 30$) and undergraduate mock jurors ($N = 47$) believed that a juvenile offender's youthful (versus adult-like) appearance would mitigate jurors' ratings of juvenile culpability. Both groups believed that jurors' perceptions of juvenile crime trends would not have an impact on culpability. In Study 2, undergraduate mock jurors ($N = 193$) read a simulated juvenile case accompanied by a photograph of a youthful versus adult-like defendant. Mock jurors who believed that juvenile crime is increasing were more likely to render guilty verdicts, but their verdicts were not affected by the juvenile's youthful appearance. Mock jurors' sentencing recommendations did not vary as a function of the juvenile's appearance or their perceptions of juvenile crime trends. Psychologists and defense attorneys may wish to emphasize the developmental immaturity of their clients to decrease their culpability to jurors, although it is unclear how large an effect this will have on verdicts and sentencing recommendations in practice.

Introduction

In 1899 a separate juvenile court system was established to try juvenile offenders apart from adult offenders (Mack, 1909). Juveniles' youthfulness was considered a mitigating factor to their culpability for their crimes (Melton, 1989). Historically, it was thought that juvenile delinquents did not understand the consequences associated with their crimes or the adult court proceedings (Cooper, 1997; Owen-Kostelnik, Reppucci, & Meyer, 2006). Juvenile cases were often tried by a judge without a jury present. However, recent legal trends allowing juveniles to be waived to adult court or tried in a hybrid juvenile/adult court in nearly every state have given adult jurors (and judges) tremendous sentencing discretion based upon the perceived culpability of juvenile defendants. For example, in Texas a jury may determine whether a juvenile defendant convicted of a first degree felony receives a sentence ranging from probation to 40 years in prison, Tex. Code Crim. Proc. Ann. art. 37.07(2)(b)(2) (Vernon Supp. 2001). Juries determine sentences for felonies in Texas and five additional states, including Virginia, Kentucky, Missouri, Arkansas, and Oklahoma (King & Noble, 2004).

A number of factors are known to affect jurors' perceptions of juvenile offender culpability, including the juvenile offenders' age (Ghetti & Redlich, 2001; Stalans & Henry, 1994), criminal history (Levine, Williams, Sixt, & Valenti, 2001; Stalans & Henry, 1994), and nature of the crime (Ghetti & Redlich, 2001). We recently had informal conversations with attorneys who work with juveniles about factors that they believed would mitigate or increase juvenile offenders' culpability in jurors' eyes. In contrast to researchers who have focused on chronological age, the attorneys felt that a youthful appearance is an important mitigating factor to adolescents' culpability. In addition, they felt that jurors who perceive that juvenile crime is increasing will view juvenile offenders' culpability more negatively than jurors who do not perceive that juvenile crime is increasing.

We conducted two studies to examine attorneys' beliefs about jurors' perceptions of juvenile culpability, whether these corresponded with jurors' perceptions of juvenile culpability, and whether juror beliefs influenced jurors' decisions in a simulated juvenile case. The first study surveyed attorneys' perceptions of factors that may mitigate an adolescent client's culpability in the eyes of potential jurors and compared their responses to the perceptions of jury-eligible college students. In our second study, we used a trial transcript accompanied by photographs to examine whether mock jurors' decisions were affected by a juvenile offender's youthful appearance and their perceptions of changes in juvenile crime rates.

Juvenile offender culpability

Applied developmental psychologists have argued that juvenile offenders are less culpable for their crimes than adults. Cognitive processes that are central to sound judgment, especially in group situations, develop during adolescence (Steinberg, 2005). Researchers contended that adolescents should be less culpable for their crimes than adults because of their diminished and still-developing decision making skills (Cauffman, Wollard, & Reppucci, 1999; Keating, 1990; Steinberg & Scott, 2003). This research has been cited in the Supreme Court's decision in *Roper v. Simmons* (2005) that ended the death penalty for juveniles as well as *Graham v. Florida* (2010) which ended sentencing juveniles to life without the possibility of parole for their crimes (e.g. Cauffman & Steinberg, 2000; Fried & Reppucci, 2001). While psychologists and the Supreme Court agree that adolescents' judgment should make them less culpable than older offenders, less is known about how jurors weigh a number of different factors when assessing juvenile culpability.

Juror perceptions of juvenile offender culpability

Jurors' assessment of adolescents' culpability is especially relevant for attorneys in Texas and five other states, where some juvenile cases are tried in front of a jury that also determines the sentencing. Several factors have been found to influence jurors' evaluations of juvenile offender culpability. For example, researchers found that mock jurors were more likely to think that a juvenile defendant with a criminal history was guilty than one who did not (Levine et al., 2001). Other researchers have found that the type of crime a juvenile committed, what the outcome of the crime was, how impulsive the juvenile was (Ghetti & Redlich, 2001), and who the victim was also mitigate juvenile offenders' culpability for their crimes (Stalans & Henry, 1994). However, less is known about how juveniles' youthful appearance and jurors' perceptions of crime trends affect their decision making.

It is well established that mock jurors generally treat chronologically older juvenile defendants more punitively than they treat younger juvenile defendants. Stalans and Henry (1994) found that mock jurors were more likely to recommend that a 16-year-old male juvenile offender be transferred to adult court than a 14-year-old male juvenile offender. Ghetti and Redlich (2001) investigated mock jurors' sentence recommendations for 11-, 14-, and 17-year-old juveniles. Mock jurors recommended longer sentences for older juvenile offenders and thought the older juvenile was more responsible and culpable for his crime than the younger juvenile. Warling and Peterson-Badali (2003) examined mock jurors' verdicts and sentence recommendations for a 13-year-old juvenile, a 17-year-old juvenile, and a 25-year-old adult offender who was accused of stabbing a same-aged peer. Mock jurors recommended longer sentences for older versus younger offenders; however, offender age did not affect verdict. Results from these studies demonstrated that jurors see juvenile offenders' age as a mitigating factor in their culpability for the crimes they have committed. In summary, mock jurors thought that younger juvenile offenders should be tried as juveniles and receive lighter sentences, and were less responsible for and less culpable for their crimes than were older juvenile offenders.

While most mock juror research has focused on the defendant's chronological age, a lack of physical maturity may be seen as being a mitigating factor, and there is some support for this from research in facial babyishness. Researchers have found that participants thought adults with babyfaced features were more honest, less likely to know right from wrong, and physically weaker than individuals with more adult-like features (Zebrowitz & McDonald, 1991; Zebrowitz & Montepare, 1992). These researchers also found that mock adult defendants in small claims court who had a babyface were perceived by mock jurors as less guilty when the crime was intentional because they perceived babyfaced defendants as more honest and naive. One limitation of the jury decision-making research on maturity is that studies have varied the described age of the juvenile in the case, but do not vary his appearance. As a result, we do not know whether 'apparent age' affects jurors' judgments in ways that are similar to or different from 'actual age.'

Only one study has looked at mock jurors' perceptions of the prevalence of juvenile crime and its effect on their perceptions of adolescent offenders' culpability (Warling & Peterson-Badali, 2003). As part of this study, Warling and Peterson-Badali (2003) had mock jurors complete their Attitude Toward Youth Crime Scale. This scale assessed participants' perceptions of whether juvenile crime was increasing or decreasing as well as participants' attitudes about punishment for juvenile offenders. The researchers found that participants who assumed juvenile crime was increasing and thought that juvenile offenders deserved harsh punishment considered juveniles to be more responsible for their crimes than did participants who did not think juvenile crime was increasing or that juvenile offenders deserved harsh punishment. However, research has not yet looked at how potential jurors' perceptions of the prevalence of juvenile crime affect their assignment of verdicts and their recommended sentences for juvenile offenders.

With some juvenile cases being tried by jurors, it is important to understand whether factors like apparent youthfulness and perceptions of crime in their area influence their views on juvenile offenders' culpability. However, attorneys' assumptions about what jurors view as mitigating factors also need to be investigated because they must develop strategies about how to present their case to the judge and jurors.

Attorney beliefs about juror perceptions of juvenile offender culpability

While researchers have examined a number of factors that might mitigate jurors' perceptions of juvenile offenders' culpability, attorneys may have slightly different ideas about what factors mitigate their adolescent clients' culpability. Juvenile defense attorneys are responsible for obtaining a not guilty verdict or the lightest sentence possible for their adolescent client (Humes, 1996). Knowledge about what factors may influence jurors' beliefs may assist with the development of trial strategy and help trial attorneys zealously advocate for their clients. Like researchers, attorneys assume that the circumstances of juvenile offenders' crimes and their history of abuse can mitigate their culpability (Dershowitz, Gill, Jouët-Nkinyangi, & Birchak, 2002). Attorneys may also present any problems the adolescent is having at school, evidence of mental retardation, and even illness as other factors that might be viewed as reducing their clients' culpability. A handbook written for juvenile defense attorneys in Texas recommends that they look for any and all circumstances and facts about their adolescent clients that may mitigate their criminal culpability (Dershowitz et al., 2002).

Viljoen and her colleagues have done several studies examining attorneys' and judges' perceptions of juvenile offenders (Viljoen, McLachlan, Wingrove, & Penner, 2010; Viljoen & Wingrove, 2007; Viljoen, Wingrove, & Ryba, 2008). Attorneys believe that an adolescent's developmental maturity is an important factor to take into consideration when he is being tried in juvenile court (Viljoen & Wingrove, 2007; Viljoen et al., 2008); however, attorneys rarely ask for competency hearings for juveniles even when they suspect that adolescents' maturity level may affect their competency to stand trial (Viljoen et al., 2010). Additionally, Viljoen and her colleagues found that attorneys and judges thought juvenile offenders' maturity level was not as important to their competency to stand trial as was the presence of mental illness (Viljoen et al., 2010). We view it as important to also examine the correspondence between attorneys' and jurors' views, as well as whether jurors' actual decision-making corresponds to their stated views.

The present studies

The present research investigated juvenile attorneys' perceptions of what factors affect potential jurors' verdicts and sentence recommendations for their adolescent clients, as well as jurors' perceptions of a juvenile offender's culpability. This research was exploratory in nature and designed to describe and compare attorneys' expectations of jurors' views of mitigating and non-mitigating factors compared to jurors' actual ratings of these factors.

We included two potentially mitigating factors in our list of items that might influence adolescent offenders' culpability in jurors' eyes but have not extensively examined. First, adolescents who look young for their chronological age may be less likely to be convicted of crimes because jurors think of these defendants as children rather than hardened criminals. Second, jurors' attitudes about current juvenile crime trends may affect their perceptions of adolescent offenders' culpability and the sentence they would recommend. Specifically, individuals who assume that juvenile crime is on the rise will be more likely to convict a juvenile defendant and will recommend a harsher sentence than will individuals who do not assume that juvenile crime is on the rise. When individuals think that juvenile crime is increasing, they may be more likely to want to recommend harsh punishment for one juvenile offender in order to deter other adolescents from committing crimes.

Study 1

In Study 1, we surveyed attorneys' beliefs about factors that may affect jurors' perceptions of juvenile offender culpability, and surveyed jury-eligible mock jurors about their personal perceptions of juvenile offender culpability. We included items found through our literature review, perusal of juvenile defense and prosecuting attorney strategy handbooks (Contreras, 2002; Dershowitz et al., 2002), and informal conversations with attorneys who have represented both the state and defendants in juvenile cases. We hypothesized that a juvenile's youthful appearance would mitigate his culpability in attorneys' perceptions of jurors' beliefs, while his adult-like appearance would not mitigate his culpability in attorneys' perceptions of jurors beliefs and mock jurors' eyes. Additionally, we hypothesized that mock jurors would report that an adolescent offender's youthful appearance would not affect their perceptions of his culpability, nor would an adolescent offender's adult-like appearance affect their perceptions of his culpability because it might not be considered socially desirable to find a person less culpable based on appearance alone.

We also hypothesized that attorneys would think that jurors' perceptions of juvenile crime trends might reduce the mitigation of a juvenile offender in jurors' eyes because jurors who follow crime trends might be more law and order oriented. We were interested in whether there might be a similar perceived lack of mitigation among jurors who followed crime trends.

Method

Participants

We sent email surveys to 381 defense and prosecuting attorneys who work with juvenile offenders or in the juvenile justice system in Texas. Juvenile attorneys from El Paso were recruited through local contacts, and additional defense and prosecuting attorneys who work with juvenile offenders or in the juvenile justice system from elsewhere in Texas were recruited through the database of the Texas State Bar website. We surveyed both defense and prosecuting attorneys who work in the juvenile justice system because we felt that both groups will have ideas about what factors influence jury decision-making and use these to formulate their trial strategies. Thirty attorneys returned completed surveys. This resulted in a response rate of 7.9%, although this may be a conservative response rate as it is not known how many attorneys actually read the email recruitment letter and surveys. On average, respondents had been practicing law for an average of 12.7 years (range 2–28 years) and had been working with juvenile offenders for an average of 8 years (range 0.5–27.5 years).

Mock jurors were 47 students enrolled in undergraduate psychology classes who received course credit for participating in the study. Participants were recruited through in-class announcements and a listing of the study on the Psychology Department's experiment participation web page for the research participant subject pool. The majority of participants were female ($n = 36$). Participants ranged in age from 18 to 45 years ($M = 23.9$, SD $= 6.5$). The makeup of the sample reflected the demographics of the university and the surrounding area. A majority of participants were Hispanic (77.1%), 10.4% were White, 2.1% were African American, 2.1% were Asian, and 4.2% were some other ethnicity or preferred not to answer.

Survey

Attorneys and mock jurors read 20 factors that could potentially be used to mitigate an adolescent offender's criminal culpability. The factors included poor school performance and behavior, family problems, socioeconomic factors, and previous delinquency. Attorneys rated how likely jurors would assume each factor mitigated a juvenile offender's culpability using a five-point Likert scale (1 = Not at all likely to mitigate adolescents' culpability in jurors' eyes, 3 = Neither likely nor unlikely to mitigate adolescents' culpability in jurors' eyes, 5 = Very likely to mitigate adolescents' culpability in jurors' eyes).

Mock jurors completed a survey packet that contained two questionnaires. The first questionnaire asked participants to categorize whether they thought the current juvenile crime trend in their community was increasing, decreasing, or staying the same, a three-choice categorical variable. After completing this initial form, participants were asked to read 20 factors that could potentially be used to mitigate an adolescent offender's criminal culpability and rate whether each item would make a juvenile more or less culpable for his actions on a five-point Likert scale. The target items, 'your perceptions of the current juvenile crime trend,' 'a juvenile's child-like appearance,' and 'a juvenile's adult-like appearance,' were embedded in this general list. Mock jurors were asked to rate the same 20 items from their own perspective, so the five-point Likert scale was reworded so that it reflected their perspective and the legal terms of 'mitigation' and 'culpability' were translated into terms appropriate for a lay audience (e.g. 5 = This makes a juvenile less responsible for his crimes, and he should receive less punishment). The target items, 'jurors' perceptions of the current juvenile crime trend,' 'a juvenile's child-like appearance,' and 'a juvenile's adult-like appearance,' were embedded in this general list.

Procedure

Attorneys received survey packets via mail or email that consisted of a letter of invitation to participate in the study, followed by the consent form and survey. When filling out the contents of the survey packet, attorneys were asked to imagine that they were defending a juvenile offender in a case where a jury would assign a verdict and sentence to the defendant.

Results

Preliminary analyses

An overall test comparing attorney's ratings of factors that might mitigate culpability in jurors' eyes to mock jurors' ratings of the same factors was conducted using a one-way MANOVA, between-groups design. This analysis found a significant multivariate effect for attorney vs mock juror groups, Wilks' lambda $= 0.34$, $F(20,55) = 5.44$, $p < 0.001$.

Attorney ratings of juror's beliefs about mitigating factors

In Table 1, we organized the data by rank ordering the factors lawyers felt were most likely to result in mitigation in jurors' eyes to least likely. The second column reflects mock jurors' ratings of the same items, and the third column contains Cohen's d difference scores between the groups. We also indicate whether the mean values are significantly different from the mid-point of 3 on the five-point scale. The hypothesis that attorneys would assume that a juvenile offender's youthful or adult-like appearance would mitigate jurors' estimations of the juvenile's culpability was supported. As hypothesized, attorneys thought that a juvenile's youthful appearance would mitigate his culpability in jurors' eyes, $M = 4.0$, while they thought that juvenile's adult-like appearance was not at all likely to mitigate his culpability in jurors' eyes, $M = 1.8$, paired $t(29) = 7.34$, $p < 0.01$. Attorneys ratings on these factors were significantly different than the mid-point value of 3 on the five-point Likert scale, $t(29) = 5.30$, $p < 0.01$ for youthful appearance, $t(29) = 5.57$, $p < 0.01$ for adult-like appearance.

The hypothesis that attorneys would think that jurors' perceptions of the crime trend would be very likely to decrease the mitigation of a juvenile offender's culpability in jurors' eyes was also supported. Attorneys thought jurors' perceptions of the current juvenile crime trend was somewhat unlikely to mitigate an adolescent's culpability in jurors' eyes, $M = 2.5$, which was significantly lower than the mid-point value on the five-point Likert scale, $t(29) = 2.39$, $p < 0.05$.

There were also several other factors that attorneys thought were important at mitigating a juvenile's culpability in jurors' eyes. Attorneys thought sexual abuse, mental retardation, child abuse and/or neglect, a mental condition, a medical condition, and violence or relational problems between family members were likely or very likely to mitigate an adolescent's culpability in jurors' eyes. There were also factors that attorneys thought were unlikely to mitigate an adolescent's culpability in jurors' eyes. Attorneys thought delinquent peers or family members, the juvenile's race/ethnicity minority status, the quality of area schools, poor school performance, use of illegal drugs, poor behavior in school, and a juvenile's gang involvement would not be likely to mitigate an adolescent's culpability.

Mock juror ratings of mitigating factors

Means and standard deviations for the juror-rated mitigating factors may be found in Table 1. We also included a t-test of the difference between juror ratings of an item and attorney ratings of an item and included Cohen's d for an estimate of the effect size of the difference between the ratings. The hypothesis that mock jurors would

Table 1. Mean and standard deviations of attorney ratings of jurors' views of mitigating factors and mock juror ratings of mitigating factors.

Factors	Attorney-rated N = 30		Mock juror-rated N = 47			Cohen's
	M	SD	M	SD	t(76)	d
Sexual abuse	4.7[b]	0.5	3.8[b]	1.4	3.45**	0.86
Mental retardation	4.6[b]	0.7	4.4[b]	1.1	0.85	0.22
Child abuse/neglect	4.5[b]	0.7	3.7[b]	1.4	3.07**	0.72
Mental condition	4.4[b]	0.9	3.8[b]	1.1	2.68**	0.60
Medical condition	4.1[b]	0.8	3.8[b]	0.9	1.57	0.35
Juvenile's child-like appearance	4.0[b]	1.0	3.5[b]	1.0	2.26*	0.50
Violence or relational problems between parents or family members	3.7[b]	1.1	3.4[a]	1.2	1.11	0.26
Family member with mental/ medical condition, substance abuse, criminal record, etc.	3.4	1.2	3.5[b]	1.1	0.55	−0.09
Lack of parental supervision	3.4	1.2	3.2	1.4	0.67	0.15
Low socio-economic status	3.1	1.1	3.5[b]	1.2	1.49	−0.35
Low socio-economic status	3.1	1.1	3.5[b]	1.2	1.49	−0.35
Neighborhood poverty, crime, economics, etc.	2.8	1.3	3.3	1.2	1.74	−0.40
Delinquent/criminal peers or family members	2.6[a]	1.1	2.8	1.2	0.88	−0.17
Jurors' perceptions of the current juvenile crime trend	2.5[a]	1.1	2.8	1.2	0.88	−0.17
Race/ethnicity	2.5[a]	1.3	3.6[b]	1.1	4.04**	−0.91
Quality of area schools	2.4[b]	1.0	3.5[b]	1.1	4.37**	−1.05
Poor school performance	2.3[b]	1.1	2.7	1.1	1.65	−0.36
Use of illegal drugs	2.0[b]	0.9	1.8[b]	1.1	0.87	0.20
Juvenile's adult-like appearance	1.8[b]	1.1	3.1	1.0	5.07**	−1.23
Poor behavior in school	1.6[b]	0.7	2.4[b]	1.1	3.52**	−0.87
Gang involvement	1.3[b]	0.7	1.6[b]	1.0	1.23	−0.35

Notes: Attorneys were asked to rate factors that jurors would view as mitigating and mock jurors were asked to rate factors that they personally felt were mitigating. Mitigation was rated on a five-point scale where 5 = *Very likely to mitigate adolescents' culpability in jurors' eyes* in the attorney-rated version and 5 = *This factor makes a juvenile less responsible for his crimes, and he should receive less punishment* in the mock juror-rated version.
*p <0.05, **p <0.01. [a]Attorney t(29) or Mock Juror t(46) significantly different from the mid-point value of 3 at p <0.05. [b]Attorney t(29) or Mock Juror t(46) significantly different from the mid-point value of 3 at p <0.01.

report that an adolescent offender's child-like or adult-like appearance would not affect their perceptions of his culpability was partly not supported. Mock jurors rated a juvenile's *adult-like appearance* as not likely to affect his responsibility for his crimes, M = 3.1, and their ratings of this factor were not significantly different from the mid-point value on this scale, t(46) = 0.39, NS. While mock jurors' rated a juvenile's youthful appearance as making a juvenile only slightly less responsible for his crimes $M = 3.5$, their ratings were significantly different from the mid-point value on this scale, $t(46) = 3.15$, $p < 0.01$. Additionally, mock jurors reported that a juvenile's *youthful appearance* would make him significantly less responsible for his crimes than would a juvenile's adult-like appearance, $d = 0.32$, paired $t(46) = 3.48$, $p < 0.01$. Mock jurors rated their perceptions of the current juvenile crime trend as not likely to affect a juvenile's responsibility for his crime, $M = 2.9$, which was not significantly different from the mid-point value on this scale, $t(46) = -0.55$, NS. Jurors' ratings of whether their knowledge of crime rates would influence their perceptions of juvenile culpability did not vary as a function of the crime trend they reported (e.g. increasing, staying the same, or decreasing), $F(2,41) = 0.38$, NS.

There were also several other factors that mock jurors rated as having a significant effect on how responsible a juvenile was for his crimes. Mock jurors rated mental retardation, sexual abuse, a mental or medical condition, child abuse/neglect, race/ethnicity, family member with mental or medical condition, or substance abuse, low socio-economic status, family violence, and quality of area schools as making a juvenile less responsible for his crimes. Mock jurors rated poor behavior in school, use of illegal drugs, and gang involvement as making a juvenile more responsible for his crimes. Thus, mock jurors saw these factors as unlikely to have a mitigating effect on a juvenile's culpability.

Compared to attorneys, mock jurors were less likely to think that sexual abuse, child abuse/neglect, mental condition, and child-like appearance would mitigate jurors' culpability judgments. In contrast, mock jurors were more likely than attorneys to think that race, quality of area schools, juvenile's adult-like appearance, and poor behavior in school would mitigate jurors' culpability judgments.

Discussion

The data strongly support the hypothesis that attorneys would think a juvenile's youthful or adult-like appearance would reduce jurors' perceptions of his culpability. Specifically, attorneys thought that a juvenile's youthful appearance would mitigate his culpability in jurors' eyes, while his adult-like appearance would not be at all likely to mitigate his culpability in jurors' eyes. The data from this study also provided some support for the hypothesis that attorneys would think jurors' perceptions of the crime trend would be likely to mitigate a juvenile offender's culpability in jurors' eyes. Attorneys thought jurors' perception of the current juvenile crime trend was somewhat more likely to not mitigate adolescent's culpability in jurors' eyes. While mock jurors reported that a juvenile offender's youthful appearance would make him slightly less culpable for his crimes, they did not report that an adult-like appearance increased culpability. Mock jurors reported that their perceptions of the juvenile crime trend would not affect their rating of the juvenile's culpability for his crimes.

It is also interesting to note that attorneys' rating of other factors that could mitigate an adolescent's criminal culpability did not match those of mock jurors in this study. For example, attorneys thought jurors would see a juvenile offender's history of sexual abuse and child abuse and neglect as being more strongly mitigating than the mock jurors did. Attorneys also viewed race/ethnicity and poor quality area schools as unlikely to be mitigating factors, but mock jurors in this study reported that both of these could be viewed as mitigating factors. This could be because a high proportion of mock jurors in our study were Hispanic in a predominantly Hispanic, economically disadvantaged city. A second study was conducted to examine whether mock jurors' behaviors would match their own perceptions and to determine whether mock jurors' behaviors were in line with attorneys' perceptions.

Study 2

In Study 2, we examined whether a juvenile offender's appearance as either youthful or adult-like affected adult jurors' verdicts and sentence recommendations. Additionally, this study explored whether mock jurors' perceptions of current juvenile crime trends affected their verdicts or sentence recommendations. Participants read a vignette that described a crime involving a juvenile offender and the ensuing trial in the determinate sentencing system and saw an accompanying photo of a youthful or adult-like 15-year-old male juvenile offender. The determinate sentencing system refers to the blended juvenile/adult system in which juveniles may start out in the juvenile system but be transferred to the adult system once they reach the age of 19 depending upon factors such as behavior while in incarceration and the nature of the offense.

We hypothesized that participants who saw a juvenile offender with a youthful appearance would be less likely to find him guilty, and recommend a less severe sentence if they thought he was guilty than participants who saw an adult-like juvenile offender. Thus, mock jurors in the present study should have been likely to assume that juvenile defendants with a youthful appearance were less culpable than juvenile defendants with an adult-like appearance. We also hypothesized that participants who thought that juvenile crime was on the rise would be more likely to find the juvenile in this case guilty, and recommend a harsher sentence if they did find him guilty than participants who thought juvenile crime was decreasing.

Method

Participants

One hundred and ninety-three undergraduate students from the psychology department's subject pool served as mock jurors in the present study. Data from 26 participants had to be discarded because those participants were less than 18 years or failed to report their age ($n = 10$) or were not jury eligible in the state of Texas because they were not registered to vote and did not have a driver's license ($n = 16$). This left data from 167 participants for subsequent analyses.

A majority (60%) of the participants were female ($n = 100$), and the proportion female did not differ significantly by condition, $\chi^2(1) = 0.07$, $p = 0.80$. Participants ranged in age from 18 to 50 years ($M = 20.7$, SD $= 4.5$). A majority of participants were Hispanic (73.3%), 12.7% were white, 4.9% were black, 4.2% were Asian, and 3.6% identified as Other.

Procedure

Undergraduate participants were recruited through the university's subject pool of psychology students and received course credit for their participation. Participants came to the lab and were asked to report whether they thought juvenile crime in their area had been increasing, decreasing, or staying the same during the past 2 years.

Participants then reviewed a juvenile case and viewed a photo of the juvenile offender. Participants read a four-page single-spaced trial transcript which included both the prosecutor and defense attorney's presentation to the court. The transcript was generated by drawing material from local cases and staging a mock trial in which a local prosecutor, defense attorney, judge, and mock witnesses delivered the testimony as naturalistically as possible, without a full script (e.g. Smith, Hosch, & Riosvelasco, 2007). Transcripts of the video were slightly modified for this case in order to obtain a high percentage of guilty verdicts because we were interested in sentencing recommendations. All participants read the same transcript about a 15-year-old male. His history of involvement with the police and juvenile justice system, the crime, the victim, and the circumstances surrounding the crime were held constant. The transcript described a school shooting that injured two students. The state presented evidence that the defendant matched the description of the gunman, knew the students who were shot, fought with one of the students a few days prior to the shooting and was later found in possession of the weapon used to commit the crime.

The transcript was further adapted for this study by having a head and shoulders photograph of the defendant appear on the first page and the top of each subsequent page. Participants saw one of three photos of a juvenile who had a youthful appearance, or one of three photos of a juvenile who had an adult-like appearance. We used multiple pictures of children matched on age to allow for heterogeneity of the stimuli on non-essential characteristics and permit stimulus generalization (Wells & Windschitl, 1999). In pilot testing, the images of youthful juveniles were estimated to be between 12.9 and 13.2 years (picture 1 had a mean age rating of 12.9 years and pictures 2 and 3 both had mean age ratings of 13.2 years), while the images of adult-like juveniles were estimated to be between 15.8 and 16.6 years (picture 4 had a mean age rating of 15.8 and pictures 5 and 6 had a mean age rating of 16.6). These images were chosen from an original sample of 16 photos of 15-year-old male adolescents and were taken by the researcher. Each adolescent was self-described Hispanic, and all shared the same hair color. Pilot participants were only asked to rate adolescents on age. The three youthful adolescent photos were chosen because they had the youngest mean age ratings, while the three adult-like adolescent photos were chosen because they had the oldest mean age ratings. A contrast of the mean ages of the three who were rated youngest versus the three who were rated oldest was highly significant $F(1,104) = 162.36$, $p < 0.0001$.

After reading the case and viewing one of the six juvenile offenders, participants gave a verdict in the case and recommended an appropriate sentence. If participants found the juvenile guilty they could recommend he be sentenced (dichotomously) to probation (6–12 months) or incarceration (1–20 years). After assigning a verdict and recommending probation or incarceration for the juvenile defendant, participants filled out a post-trial questionnaire to assess what information they remembered from the trial transcript and a demographic form.

Results

Verdicts

Preliminary analyses found that 94.0% of participants determined that the juvenile defendant was guilty ($n = 157$). The hypothesis that a juvenile's appearance would affect participants' verdicts was not supported. Participants were no more likely to find an adult-like juvenile offender guilty than they were to find a youthful juvenile offender guilty, $\chi^2(1) = 0.00$, NS. The hypothesis that participants' perceptions that the juvenile crime was increasing would affect their verdicts was supported, $\chi^2(1) = 4.08$, $p < 0.05$, $\theta = 0.16$. Over half of participants (52.9%) who determined the defendant guilty thought juvenile crime in their community was increasing. Participants who thought that the crime trend was increasing were more likely to determine that the juvenile was guilty than were participants who thought the crime trend was staying about the same or decreasing (increasing $= 97.5\%$, staying the same or decreasing $= 90.0\%$). Of the participants who determined the defendant was not guilty, 20.0% thought juvenile crime in their community was increasing, and 80.0% thought crime was staying about the same or decreasing.

Sentence recommendations

Of the 153 participants who determined the juvenile was guilty, 33.3% ($n = 51$) recommended he be sentenced to some period of probation, while 66.7% ($n = 102$) recommended he be sentenced to some period of incarceration. The hypothesis that a juvenile defendant's appearance would affect participants' sentence recommendations was not supported, $\chi^2(1) = 0.62$, NS. The hypothesis that participants' perceptions of the juvenile crime trend would affect their sentence recommendations was also not supported, $\chi^2(1) = 0.12$, NS.

Discussion

Contrary to our hypotheses, there were no significant differences between the verdicts of mock jurors who saw a youthful juvenile offender and those who saw an adult-like juvenile offender. There were also no significant differences between sentence recommendations (probation vs incarceration) of mock jurors who saw a youthful juvenile offender compared to those who saw an adult-like juvenile offender. The data supported the hypothesis that jurors who thought juvenile crime was increasing would be more likely to find the juvenile offender guilty and would recommend he receive a more severe punishment than mock jurors who thought the crime trend was staying the same or decreasing. Specifically, jurors who thought the juvenile crime trend was increasing were significantly more likely to determine that the juvenile offender was guilty than jurors who thought the juvenile crime trend was stable or decreasing. However, there were no significant differences among the sentence recommendations (probation vs incarceration) of mock jurors who thought the crime trend was increasing or not.

General discussion

Our findings from Study 1 supported the hypotheses that attorneys would think that a juvenile's youthful appearance would mitigate his culpability in jurors' eyes, while a juvenile's adult-like appearance would be unlikely to mitigate his culpability in jurors' eyes. Also consistent with our hypothesis, attorneys thought that jurors' perceptions of the current juvenile crime trend as trending upward would somewhat increase a juvenile offender's culpability in jurors' eyes. Consistent with attorneys' views, our survey of mock jurors found that a child-like appearance could be viewed as a mitigating factor. Attorneys' and mock jurors' stated views that youthful appearance may be a mitigating factor is related to recent findings that judges and attorneys think a juvenile offender's developmental maturity is an important factor influencing his culpability (Viljoen & Wingrove, 2007; Viljoen et al., 2008). These findings are also consistent with an attorney's observation that jurors will rarely send adolescent offenders to prison when their feet do not reach the floor while they sit at the defense table in court (D. R. Contreras, personal communication, July 2007). The finding of perceptions of lessened culpability for a youthful appearance may play a role in how attorneys present their case. They may choose to dress their client in ways that emphasize a youthful appearance or emphasize their client's youthfulness and immaturity when they have an opportunity to do so in opening and closing arguments. However, when mock jurors were given a trial transcript with pictures of youthful or adult-looking 15-year-olds in Study 2, there was no difference in mock jurors' verdicts and sentence recommendations. Further research may be necessary to determine whether factors such as the violent nature of the crime in our scenario in Study 2 may have overridden the effects of the defendant's youthfulness. Given our equivocal findings regarding juvenile defendants' youthfulness, defense attorneys may want to play up a defendant's youthful appearance to gain sympathy from the jurors as it is more likely to be helpful to this than harmful.

Taken as a whole, the results from these studies demonstrate that what attorneys think are important mitigating factors for their adolescent clients may or may not correspond to what jurors see as important mitigating factors for an adolescent offender in both their expressed views and their actions. Our finding that jurors who thought that crime was increasing were more likely to convict is consistent with attorneys' views and prior research on mock juror punitiveness (Warling & Peterson-Badali, 2003). Based on our findings, defense attorneys may want to ask prospective jurors about their thoughts on the current juvenile crime trend in *voir dire* because mock jurors who do not think that crime is increasing may be more receptive to defense arguments. In contrast, prosecuting attorneys may want to focus on jurors who think the crime rate is increasing in order to find jurors who will to send a message to the community that adolescents who behave this way will be punished.

The studies presented here demonstrate that attorneys' assumptions of what factors affect a juvenile offender's culpability in jurors' eyes may differ from jurors' perceptions. Research in this area of legal psychology is important for attorneys, judges, and offenders. Determining what jurors see as important mitigating factors to an adolescent's culpability may allow attorneys to know what factors may help increase or decrease the perception of an adolescent offender's culpability. Our findings also highlight the importance for attorneys to use focus groups (when feasible) and the *voir dire* process in order to learn about jurors' attitudes rather than making assumptions about them. Jury decisions in juvenile cases are likely to be somewhat different from judges' decisions, as jurors are not exposed to juvenile defendants on a day-to-day basis. Because of the tremendous latitude jurors have in determining sentences in some states, some form of guidance for jurors may be helpful to allow them to get a sense of what an appropriate sentence might be for juveniles convicted of particular crimes.

Limitations and future directions

One limitation to our study is the low response rate from attorneys, as we do not know whether the attorneys who responded to our survey are similar to or different from nonresponding attorneys and attorneys more generally. Another limitation is that we included both prosecuting and defense attorneys in our survey of attorneys who work with juveniles. While attorneys who work on both sides of juvenile cases may have ideas about what factors are important for jurors and use these when developing a trial strategy, defense and prosecution attorneys may nonetheless vary in their emphasis of different mitigating factors. As many juvenile cases remain in juvenile court are tried before judges, it would be interesting to see how their views on mitigation are similar or different from those of attorneys and jurors. All of these remain unanswered empirical questions that may be addressed by future research.

Future research might incorporate a larger variety of dependent measures, as defendant youthfulness and perceptions of crime trends might affect a range of judgments affecting verdict and sentencing decisions. Furthermore, a manipulation of crime severity and defendant youthfulness might reveal whether the youthful appearance may be more of an advantage with less serious crimes rather than violent crimes.

Recent research has demonstrated that jurors' individual characteristics may be more predictive of their criminal justice decisions than are factors related to the case (Walker & Woody, 2011). In one recent study, Walker and Woody (2011)) found that pro-prosecution mock jurors were more likely to find an offender guilty regardless of whether the offender was portrayed as a juvenile or an adult than mock jurors who did not have a pro-prosecution bias. It would also be interesting to learn whether juror's perceptions of the crime trend were related to their bias toward the legal system, such as those assessed by the Juror Bias Scale (Warling & Peterson-Badali, 2003). Perhaps a juror's perception of the crime trend is a specific factor related to the overarching construct of the juror's bias toward the legal system. Understanding whether a juror's perceptions of the crime trend are related to bias may allow researchers to more accurately understand why perceptions of the crime trend would affect jurors' verdicts and sentence recommendations.

We found few variations in jurors' verdicts and sentence recommendation between youthful and adult-like juvenile offenders. This may have been due to the trial transcript which described a violent crime and was designed to obtain a high proportion of guilty verdicts in order to assess variations in sentencing recommendations. The use of a more ambiguous fact pattern would allow for more variations in jurors' verdicts and sentence recommendations and could possibly allow jurors' beliefs about crime trends and evaluation of the youthful appearance of the offender to play a larger role. This study also focused upon Hispanic male offenders in a predominantly Hispanic community. Whether or not our findings generalize to cases involving defendants of a different ethnic group from the jury members or female juvenile offenders remains to be addressed empirically and should be a topic for future research.

The findings from these studies have several implications for the legal field. The present research can assist attorneys who work with juvenile offenders in preparing their cases by demonstrating which potential mitigating factors may have the most affect on jurors. These findings also demonstrate that attorneys' beliefs about the factors that may mitigate a juvenile offender's culpability in jurors eyes may not always be what actually affects jurors' perceptions of a juvenile offender's culpability. Finally, while we did not find that mock jurors were influenced by the appearance of babyfaced juvenile defendants, those that believed that juvenile crime is increasing were more likely to find the juvenile defendant guilty.

References

Cauffman, E., Wollard, J., & Reppucci, N.D. (1999). Justice for juveniles: New perspectives on adolescents' competence and culpability. *Quinnipiac Law Review, 18,* 403–420.

Cauffman, E., & Steinberg, L. (2000). (Im)maturity of judgment in adolescence: Why adolescents may be less culpable than adults. *Behavioral Sciences & the Law, 18*(6), 741–760. doi:10.1002/bsl.416

Contreras, D. (2002). *An overview of juvenile law and the elected prosecutor's role.* Unpublished manuscript.

Cooper, D.K. (1997). Juveniles' understanding of trial-related information: Are they competent defendants? *Behavioral Sciences and the Law, 15,* 167–180. doi:10.1002/ (SICI)1099-0798(199721)15:2 < 167::AID-BSL266 > 3.0.CO;2-E

Dershowitz, H.L., Gill, R., Jouët-Nkinyangi, M., & Birchak, F. (2002). *Juvenile practice is not child's play: A handbook for attorneys who represent juveniles in Texas.* Austin, TX: Texas Appleseed.

Fried, C.S., & Reppucci, N. (2001). Criminal decision making: The development of adolescent judgment, criminal responsibility, and culpability. *Law and Human Behavior, 25*(1), 45–61. doi:10.1023/A:1005639909226

Ghetti, S., & Redlich, A.D. (2001). Reactions to youth crime: Perceptions of accountability and competency. *Behavioral Sciences and the Law, 19,* 33–52. doi:10.1002/bsl.426

Graham v. Florida: 560 U.S. ___ (2010).

Humes, E. (1996). *No matter how loud I shout: A year in the life of juvenile court.* New York, NY: Touchstone.

Keating, D. (1990). Adolescent thinking. In S.S. Feldman & G.R. Elliot (Eds.), *At the threshold: The developing adolescent* (pp. 54–89). Cambridge, MA: Harvard University.

King, N.J., & Noble, R.J. (2004). Felony jury sentencing in practice: A three-state study. *Vanderbilt Law Review, 57,* 885–962.

Levine, M., Williams, A., Sixt, A., & Valenti, R. (2001). Is it inherently prejudicial to try a juvenile as an adult? *Behavioral Sciences and the Law, 19,* 23–31. doi:10.1002/bsl.428

Mack, J. (1909). The juvenile court. *Harvard Law Review, 23,* 104–115.

Melton, G.B. (1989). Taking *Gault* seriously: Toward a new juvenile court. *Nebraska Law Review, 68,* 146–181.

Owen-Kostelnik, J., Reppucci, N.D., & Meyer, J.R. (2006). Testimony and interrogation of minors: Assumptions about maturity and morality. *American Psychologist, 61,* 286–304. doi:10.1037/0003–066X.61.4.286

Roper v. Simmons, 543 U.S. 551 (2005).

Smith, B.A., Hosch, H.M., & Riosvelasco, T. (2007, May). *Beyond a reasonable doubt: The influence of language of testimony on the Reasonable Doubt Standard.* Poster presented at the Annual Western Psychological Association Conference, Vancouver: BC.

Stalans, L.J., & Henry, G.T. (1994). Societal views of justice for adolescents accused of murder: Inconsistency between sentiment and automatic legislative transfers. *Law and Human Behavior, 18,* 675–696. doi:10.1007/BF01499331

Steinberg, L. (2005). Cognitive and affective development in adolescence. *Trends in Cognitive Sciences, 9,* 69–74. doi:10.1016/j.tics.2004.12.005

Steinberg, L., & Scott, E.S. (2003). Less guilty by reason of adolescence: Developmental immaturity, diminished responsibility, and the juvenile death penalty. *American Psychologist, 58,* 1009–1018. doi:10.1037/0003-066X.58.12.1009

Tex. Code Crim. Proc. Ann. art. 37.07(2)(b)(2) (Vernon Supp. 2001).

Viljoen, J., McLachlan, K., Wingrove, T., & Penner, E. (2010). Defense attorneys' concerns about the competence of adolescent defendants. *Behavioral Sciences and the Law, 28,* 30–646. doi:10.1002/bsl.954

Viljoen, J., & Wingrove, T. (2007). Adjudicative competence in adolescent defendants: Judges' and defense attorneys' views of legal standards for adolescents in juvenile and criminal court. *Psychology, Public Policy, and Law, 13,* 204–229. doi:10.1037/1076–8971.13.3.204

Viljoen, J., Wingrove, T., & Ryba, N.L. (2008). Adjudicative competence evaluations of juvenile and adult defendants: Judges' views regarding essential components of competence reports. *International Journal of Forensic Mental Health, 7,* 107–119. doi:10.1080/14999013.2008.9914408

Walker, C.M., & Woody, W.D. (2011). Juror decision making for juveniles tried as adults: The effects of defendant age, crime type, and crime outcome. *Psychology, Crime & Law, 17,* 659–675. doi:10.1080/10683160903493471

Warling, D., & Peterson-Badali, M. (2003). The verdict on jury trials for juveniles: The effects of defendant's age on trial outcomes. *Behavioral Sciences and the Law, 21,* 63–82. doi:10.1002/bsl.517

Wells, G.L., & Windschitl, P.D. (1999). Stimulus sampling and social psychological experimentation. *Personality and Social Psychology Bulletin, 25,* 1115–1125. doi:10.1177/01461672992512005

Zebrowitz, L.A., & McDonald, S.M. (1991). The impact of litigants' baby-facedness and attractiveness on adjudications in small claims court. *Law and Human Behavior, 15,* 603–623. doi:10.1007/BF01065855

Zebrowitz, L.A., & Montepare, J.M. (1992). Impressions of babyfaced individuals across the life span. *Developmental Psychology, 28,* 1143–1152. doi:10.1037/0012-1649.28.6.1143

Index

INDEX